GHOSTS
OF THE PAST

Adelaide Gaol entrance.

GHOSTS OF THE PAST

One Paranormal Team's Experiences In The Adelaide Gaol

Alison Oborn

Notes:
A plan of the Gaol can be found on page xi

Abbreviations:
    P.F.I.   Paranormal Field Investigators
    EMF   Electro Magnetic Field
    EVP   Electronic Voice Phenomena

Published privately in 2010 by Alison Oborn and
              Paranormal Field Investigators
c/- Post Office
One Tree Hill
South Australia   5114
www.paranormalfieldinvestigators.com

Second editon published 2013.

Photography by Alison Oborn

Copyright © Alison Oborn
No reproduction without permission

Oborn, Alison, 1962–
Title Details
Title 1 of 1 - Ghosts of the Past
Subtitle: One Paranormal Team's Experiences in the Adelaide Gaol

ISBN 978-0-646-53858-7

Wholly produced and set up in Adelaide, South Australia
Designed and typeset by Pamela and Ben Oborn
Printed by Digital Print Australia, 135 Gilles Street, Adelaide, SA 5000

Distributed by Adelaide's Haunted Horizons
www.adelaidehauntedhorizons.com.au

CONTENTS

Foreword		vi
Author's Preface		viii
Acknowledgements		ix
Chapter 1	The Early Days	1
Chapter 2	The Hunt Begins	17
Chapter 3	Let the Show go on	27
Chapter 4	A Night to Remember	39
Chapter 5	A Finished Hiatus	53
Chapter 6	The Ghost Tours Continue	69
Chapter 7	Winds of Change	79
Chapter 8	Worries and Workshops	89
Chapter 9	A New Beginning	103
Chapter 10	Back at Last	111
Chapter 11	A New Chapter in Experiments	116
Chapter 12	What of the Future?	131
Chapter 13	A Final Farewell	139
Bibliography		154

FOREWORD

ALISON Oborn and I first became friends early in the year 2008, when we began communicating with each other online. What initially sparked our communication with each other was our mutual interest in the paranormal. Alison, along with her co-founder Jeff, were the founders of Paranormal Field Investigators based in Adelaide, South Australia, while my wife Sandra and I were the founders of New England Anomalies Research based in Rhode Island, USA. As my regular discussions with Alison about various paranormal topics continued, I found her to be an extremely intelligent and well-spoken person, and her practical approach to paranormal research and investigation was an attribute that both Sandra and I greatly admired.

One of the topics Alison and I discussed, which I found of particular interest, was of her and her team's ongoing investigations at the Old Adelaide Gaol in South Australia, a place that had functioned as a major prison for well over a century, and which now serves as a popular local tourist attraction. Prior to my friendship with Alison, I had never heard of the Old Adelaide Gaol, and I readily became intrigued by Alison's stories about this institution's fascinating and macabre history. Not surprisingly, the Gaol was rumoured to be haunted. I was further intrigued to learn that Alison and her team had spent six years thoroughly researching and documenting the haunting activity within the Old Adelaide Gaol. In fact, the Gaol often served as their own personal 'laboratory', as Alison referred to it, where they could conduct ongoing research within a location, which appeared rife with unexplained phenomena!

And what place could be more suitable for possible haunting phenomena, than the Old Adelaide Gaol? With over forty executions having taken place in its long history (one being a woman), combined with the fact that many of these condemned inmates were given an impersonal final resting place within the Gaol's very walls, it was certainly no wonder that so many frightening occurrences were reported there! Literally thousands of inmates were incarcerated in this labyrinth-like building over the years, and it was certainly the setting of untold sufferings for these unfortunate prisoners.

As Alison shared more and more details with me about what she, Jeff and their team mates had personally experienced at the Gaol, I realized that there was quite a story here. I promptly invited Alison to appear on an episode of our local paranormal TV talk show called *Ghosts R N.E.A.R.*, which was hosted by Sandra and myself, should she ever be willing to share her story with an American television audience.

The opportunity for Alison to be interviewed on our show, live and in person, presented itself during the last week of August in 2008, when Alison found herself visiting with us here in Rhode Island as our guest. Almost immediately after her arrival – despite suffering from more than 24 hours sleep deprivation, on top of fighting off a migraine headache – Alison appeared on Ghosts R N.E.A.R., and shared her fascinating story with us in front of a live TV audience. And she was absolutely wonderful!

Naturally, I thereafter began encouraging Alison to utilize her story-telling talents by putting her adventures relating to the Old Adelaide Gaol into book form… an idea which she herself had been toying with for some time. And now, I am very excited that this idea has now become a reality!

What follows is not only the history of a vast historic prison, its gruesome history and its many unusual happenings, it is also the fascinating true story of a small yet close-knit group of talented individuals, and especially of one woman's incredible determination, to uncover the truth behind any possible haunting phenomena within the darkened recesses of the Old Adelaide Gaol. I heartily encourage you to join in the adventure as Alison and her team members initially confront the phenomena, deal with numerous setbacks and other obstacles, and ultimately meet with the thrill of discovery.

I've no doubt that you will be as captivated with this true-to-life adventure as I have been!

Keith Johnson

Former cast member of Syfy's *Ghost Hunters*
Co-founder of N.E.A.R

AUTHOR'S PREFACE

"WHY write a book on the paranormal?" I hear you ask. "Don't we already have enough out there?"

Well… yes, we have lots of books out there! Each day a new one springs up, some good and some… well in reality, should never have hit the printers! Hopefully you will consider this book to be in the first category, or at least somewhere in-between. I have written this book through my passion for the Adelaide Gaol and for the paranormal research work our team has done there. We spent so many years there, that we couldn't help but fall in love with her, like many others have done before us. In fact so much so, that I wanted to give back something to thank her: and so it was that I stayed on as a volunteer and still continue to raise money through helping to conduct the Ghost Tours. I wanted to write this book as a record of Paranormal Field Investigators' (P.F.I.) involvement there; also to pay tribute to her, and in so doing so maybe help you to appreciate her a little more and encourage you to visit yourself.

Please note that this book was NEVER meant to be a methodology or 'how to' book, for if I was to put down every detail on how we did it and dwelled on instrument readings, many of you, the readers would never get passed Chapter Two… or maybe Three! This is meant for your enjoyment only. It is for those out there who enjoy reading about a good ghost story and for those who are intrigued to know more about what happens behind her walls after the lights go down. I will relate these experiences here: they all happened, they were all very real to those who experienced them at the time – but it will be up to you, the reader, to make of them what you will. After all the phenomena that we term 'paranormal' is not a proven science.

Some names have been changed in this book, purely to protect the identity and privacy of the people involved. Where real names have been added it has been with permission, or only first names used. Where conversations are used, these too are rough conversations held on the night to make the stories flow.

Being a keen photographer, and as the Gaol presents such a unique subject, I also wanted to make this book an acknowledgement of her beauty, so have also included a pictorial tribute to her. They are not paranormal photographs, as many of our photos we have now found natural explanations to. Hopefully though, by including these building photographs it will help give you a feel for the Old Girl that we are all so very fond of.

ACKNOWLEDGEMENTS

I would like to thank the staff of the Department of Environment and Heritage, we thank them and their management at the Gaol, especially Deanne Hanchant-Nicholls, for allowing us the freedom to investigate and the trust they have given us in doing so for all these years.

Of course there are my friends overseas who in the early stages encouraged me to keep writing and without whom I would have given up, and nearly did several times. In particular I would like to thank Keith and Carl Johnson for not only their friendship but also their inspiration too; they have helped me to believe in myself, and for that I am always grateful.

I would also like to thank Karen at the Gaol and especially my in-laws, Pamela and Ben Oborn, for proofreading, typesetting and helping get this book to the publisher. It was all very confusing and without this help it probably would still just be sitting on my hard-drive gathering dust.

It is at this point I would like to give HUGE thanks to the volunteer members of Paranormal Field Investigators, for without their hard work and enthusiasm these stories could never be told. A research group is only as strong as the members in it, and the present team especially, is something to be incredibly proud of. So thanks go to Anna Bird, Megan Pannell, Spilios Zogopoulos and Brett Burford, Debbie Jackson and Amy… also to our past members Bill, Patrick and, of course, Jeff amongst others.

Finally, and most importantly, I would like to thank my family who have been incredibly patient as I take off once more for an investigation or tour. To Michael, my husband, who for all these years has watched his hard-earned money being channelled into really important items such as another voice recorder or a new IR video camera: I thank you. For all those years that you stayed at home and 'bonded' with our children whilst I disappeared once again in an evening: I thank you again. To Rebecca and Cameron, our two children, I would like to thank you for making my life complete. For being fine about my absence, and for your love that you give in return: I thank you both too. You are my life and I am very proud of you both.

And now, on with the stories…

x

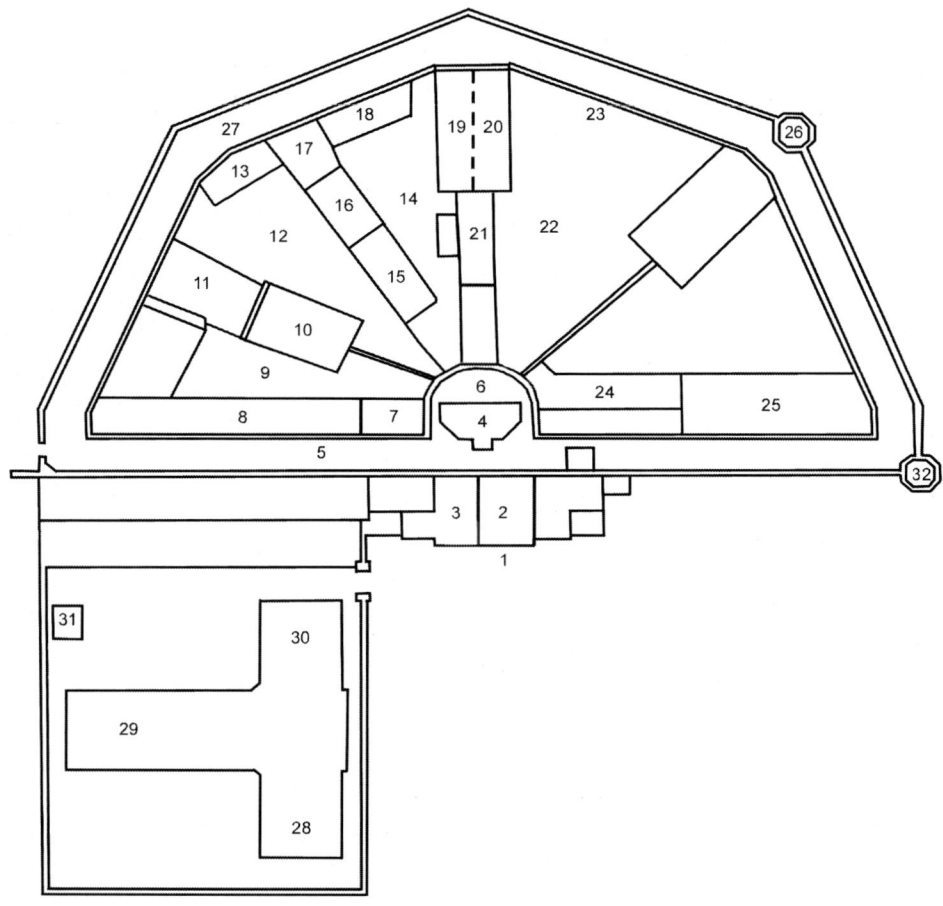

1. Adelaide Gaol Main Entrance
2. Sallyport
3. Shop
4. Visitors Centre
5. Laneway
6. Turning Circle
7. Medical Centre
8. Upstairs Dormitories
9. Yard 1
10. Cell Block
    / Elizabeth Woolcock Display
11. Kitchen
12. Yard 2
13. Toilet Block
14. Yard 3
15. Clothing Store
16. Induction Centre
17. Recreation Room
18. Old Kitchen/Education Centre
20. Yard 4 Cell block
21. Old Cell blocks/Canteen
22. Yard 4
23. Porta-cabin (no longer there)
24. Remand/Museum
25. Remand Cell block
26. Hanging Tower
27. Cemetery/Portable Gallows
28. New Building 'A' Wing
29. New Building 'B' Wing
30. New Building 'C' Wing
31. New Building Yard Toilets
32. Guard's Tower

Map drawn and compiled by Michael and Rebecca Oborn

xi

Guard's Tower after a storm

Chapter 1
The Early Days

paranormal, adj. *outside normal knowledge or perception…*
ghost, n. *the disembodied spirit of a dead person imagined as wandering among or haunting living persons…*
haunt, v.t. *to reappear frequently to after death; visit habitually as a supposed spirit or ghost…*

(Macquarie Dictionary)

OUR group, known as Paranormal Field Investigators (P.F.I.), was formed in January 2002. Although we were the 'new kids on the block', experience was certainly not lacking in the team. Many of its members had cut their teeth and done their time in various other groups prior to joining P.F.I. Two team members had even lived in 'haunted' houses as children, and one of these members still did.

I was one of those who had been born into a haunted house, a house that had many strange things happen within its walls. This house had terrified me and for many years had been the cause of my sleeping with my bedroom lights on. In fact this was a nightly occurrence leading right up into my 20s. But, like a moth to a flame, I was drawn to the subject and throughout my life had researched and dabbled in various aspects of the phenomenon. It wasn't until I immigrated to Australia in 1989 that my fascination with the subject blossomed and I finally joined various teams in both the UFO and the paranormal investigation fields.

It was during this time also that I met Jeff, both of us having joined a new team at roughly the same time. With both of us having the unfamiliarity with this new team in common, it was only natural that we would form a friendship. We shared many experiences during this period, but soon found ourselves becoming more and more frustrated as avenues of research that we wanted to follow couldn't be tested under the constraints of the team we were in at the time.

"Maybe we should set up our own team?" Jeff suggested one evening, setting his glass down and looking across at me. By this time both Jeff and I had finally resigned from the team and now were in limbo when it came to investigation work.

I thought about the implications of this for a moment. "Well at least that way, we could take the investigation work in the direction we have always wanted to go with it," I agreed.

The biggest problem we could foresee was where we would find reliable team members. We needn't have worried though, as word very quickly spread that a new team had formed. First came Bill, a colleague of Jeff's, and for a while the three of us tried out various techniques, and learnt by the mistakes we made along the way. Members of the previous group closely followed, after having tracked us down and requested to join also. One of these was Megan Pannell, a professional photographer, whom we had come to know well; closely followed by Patrick, whose electronic skills were more than welcomed. In time others joined and things were starting to look up for the team.

So it was in January 2002, Paranormal Field Investigators was finally born!

—000—

My first ever visit to the Adelaide Gaol had been with my previous team when we had been booked in on the Ghost Tour that was regularly held there. We had heard the rumours that it was 'haunted', but had found no real reference to this in any literature. Certainly no paranormal team had ever been into this building to see if this could be verified in any way.

So it was on this tour that I found myself standing in awe of the sheer magnificence of this old building. It was a place steeped in history, a history that could still be felt and sensed all around. The feeling only grew as we were taken around by our tour guide, Trevor. Trevor had a wealth of knowledge on the Gaol, not only on its history but also on its ghostly stories. It was particularly effective because Trevor himself had worked at the Gaol when it was still operating under Correctional Services.

It was also on this tour that I got to experience what the Gaol possibly had on offer for myself…a first taste that only proved to wet my appetite all the more to get in to investigate this place properly.

Hanging back from the tour party, I had been concentrating on acquiring video footage in the vain hope I might capture something unusual whilst there. It wasn't far into the tour that we entered Yard 2 and patiently listened to stories told from within, whilst looking up at the tallest cellblock in the Gaol. Being three storeys high, it was quite an imposing building, but one that nobody was allowed to enter due to safety reasons. It was as we were led further into this yard that the atmosphere began to change.

Although no ghostly tales were told about the old kitchen that silently stood in the corner of Yard 2, something drew me to it. Wandering over to the large gate-like door, I tested the handle to see if I could get a sneak peak inside. Locked! I bent down and peered through the opening on the gate and into its black interior. Yes, plenty of room to push a camcorder through, I decided. Switching on the infra-red mode I viewed the empty room within on the LCD screen – a room that seemed normal, although dirty from years of disuse. So, why were tentacles of dread starting to wrap themselves around me? After all there had been no stories told of this building, no macabre tales, and no startling accounts in history; but still the unease grew. 'It's OK,' I told myself, 'I am not alone, and imagination is probably just getting the better of me'. I would suggest that most human beings have a natural fear of dark spaces and areas. It is inbuilt into us all, a survival technique dating back to our days of living round the campfires. Not being nocturnal by nature, we have poor eyesight in the dark, and this is where predators and enemies would lurk and be in their element. Our hesitation and fear of the dark would certainly have kept us safe, keeping us close to the light of our fires or locked in our dwellings.

As I stood at that gate the feeling only heightened; but it was now being accompanied by a much stronger sensation, one that warned me that something dark and menacing was rushing towards me. Could I see anything? No, I just sensed it. Imagination? Possibly. But for me at that moment it was a very real feeling and all my protective instincts kicked in. Wrenching the camera back out of the small opening I had jammed it in, and with my heart pounding, I started slowly backing up. Swinging around I eagerly looked to join the safety of the group once more, only to find that I now stood alone in a silent, darkened yard, the tour having moved off moments earlier. My flight instinct finally kicked in and I raced into the adjoining yard and back into the comfort of the tour group. The out-takes on my video camera, however, were a sight to behold, having forgotten to turn it off in my panic!

We continued to weave our way through the Gaol, admiring the old buildings as we passed them by, shivering in the cold at the eerie stories being told, and all the while I still hung back from the tour…but now maybe, not quite as far. It wasn't long before we stepped out onto a cement path which wound its way to a building we had all been anticipating: it was the path that led to the Hanging

Tower. As the tour approached the solemn building and stepped into the darkness within, I decided once more to keep walking a short distance behind the tour and soon found myself standing alongside a wall which had numbers and letters stencilled onto it. I had found the graves and all that remained to show where the executed still lay in their last resting place. It was then that I stood and did something I wouldn't contemplate doing today: I 'dared them'! If there was something there, then "go on… I dare you to try something!" I stood silently with only my misty breathe for company and the sound of my breathing punctuating the air. Nothing. Sighing, and with a feeling of disappointment, I turned back to the Tower and rejoined the group to listen to the stories of the hangings. It was as I stood back in the Tower I noticed that the coach driver, who was standing in the far corner against the wall, was starting to look agitated. He had paled, looking almost sweaty and had started rubbing at the back of his neck. Suddenly he broke away from the tour and hurried down the metal walkway leading from the Tower and slumped down at the end, head in hands. I quickly followed him, to make sure he was OK.

"I felt a tightening around the back of my neck," he explained, "and a pain just to one side as if I had a noose around my neck". With that he took a deep breathe and went quiet. Psychosomatic… was this a possible explanation to what he had been feeling? After all we had been talking about hangings and our brains do work in strange and mysterious ways. The metal walkway clanged, startling us both, and I was soon joined by other concerned members of the tour. Feeling that there were now more than enough people to take care of this shaken man, I left and re-entered the Tower. I continued to listen to the tales and watched as finally the tour group left, picking up the coach driver along the way.

A girl from the tour glanced my way as she was leaving and noticed I was not about to depart the Tower any time soon. Having also witnessed what had just happened to the coach driver, she sauntered back over to the corner I had now positioned myself in. There we both stood with only the darkness for company. Nothing untoward appeared to be happening and soon we started to forget the supernatural and started to chat to each other on other more mundane topics.

It was then she looked at me curiously: "Are you OK?" she asked.

I wasn't sure, for suddenly I had been taken by surprise as a strange sensation had swept over me. A pressure had started to press into my back which I was starting to feel internally. My kidneys ached, my stomach ached and rolled producing waves of nausea, and I was finding it increasingly hard to breathe. The surprise and discomfort must have been reflected on my face as the girl, becoming concerned, seized my arm and started to pull me out of the Hanging Tower. It was as we finally hit the end of the metal walkway that the feeling lifted completely and once more I felt fine. 'Well that will teach me,' I concluded, 'maybe in future I will refrain from challenging them'.

And so it was that a strong interest in the Gaol had blossomed. I now had a taste of what she possibly had on offer should we ever be allowed back in, this time to investigate. A longing to do so was growing deep inside.

A BRIEF HISTORY OF THE ADELAIDE GAOL

Before relating any more of these experiences, some notes on the history of the Gaol will, I hope, put the events into context.

"What is the meaning of this Sir? Explain to us WHY you felt the need to use this money to build such an elaborate Gaol? You are a free colony Sir, you have no convicts!"

One can only imagine the conversation that went on between Governor Gawler and the Authorities back in England: he had nearly bankrupted the Colony of South Australia with the building of Her Majesty's Adelaide Gaol, along with expenditure on other projects such as Parliament House. But nearly bankrupt it he did, and he was soon called back to England to answer the questions that were raised.

The idea behind the settlement of South Australia was unlike the rest of this new land, in that it would be colonised by free people. People who had not been convicted of any crime. People who were keen, for whatever reason, to start a new life; so much so that they were prepared to leave behind family and friends to follow this dream. They had been told a grand new life could be had out there, where a man could make something of himself… a new land of opportunities.

However, they were also living on a continent largely populated by transported convicts. These prisoners, who although they were sent to other areas of the country, often escaped and travelled across the land. The fear was strong that these convicts would make their way down to South Australia, and often they did. This fear was so great that South Australia was the first colony in the whole of Australia to implement a police force.

Ghosts of the Past

Of course where you have growing numbers of people, crime will naturally follow and this was no different for South Australia. At first prisoners were kept confined on a ship, the HMS *Buffalo*, but soon, as the ship was recalled for duty, a new place for these people had to be found. A tent was erected on the banks of the Torrens and for a time they were even chained to logs. This was closely followed by a wooden hut, which also proved to be just as ineffective as often these prisoners would escape. A new solution was needed, and so it was that tenders went out to construct a new gaol.

Work eventually started on HM Adelaide Gaol, designed by George Strickland Kingston and based on the design of Pentworth Prison back in the UK. The building commenced in 1840 and the doors finally opened a year later, ready to receive the influx of prisoners that at first didn't come. In fact for many years locals complained that this Gaol was nothing but an eyesore; a blemish that ate a large part of South Australia's budget. At first the costing was around £17,000 to £19,000: however, changes were made and parts added, and before long that cost rose. A visitor to Adelaide noted that: "£34,000 has been thrown away, ornamented with a parcel of trumpery and useless towers ... containing accommodation for 140 imaginary prisoners."

But the Gaol was now here to stay; and so it was that William Baker Ashton was appointed the first Governor of the Adelaide Gaol – which was often referred to as 'Ashton's Hotel'. At this stage the Gaol was only half built, but it was viewed functional enough to begin her working life.

To start with business was slow: but as the years went by it was a case of 'build it and they will come', and Governor Gawler's foresight ended up silencing his detractors. Eventually the Gaol expanded and grew, and the second half of the original plan was built in 1847/48.

Although to start with the Gaol was attracting on average two prisoners a month, it soon started to fill up. During its years of service an estimated 300,000 men, women and sometimes children passed through its doors. In the early days prisoners were categorised as either felons or debtors; but no thought was given to breaking these categories down any further. People waiting for judgement were kept with criminals; the mentally insane were put with debtors, and men and women were thrown together. As time went on this slowly changed and the women were finally separated from the men – although it was stated that the guards were often more of a problem to them than the male prisoners!

The Early Days

The Governor's Quarters above the Sallyport

It is said that approximately three hundred people died within the prison walls over this time. Not only were people executed: there also was disease, violence and natural causes at play in the attainment of such a number. But it will always be the 45 executed prisoners who will be at the fore of the deaths remembered in this Gaol.

Between 1840 and 1964, one woman and 44 men were hanged at the Adelaide Gaol in four separate areas. Portable gallows were used for 20 of these people; a further 21 were hanged in the New Building, and four in the Hanging Tower. All of their bodies remain buried within the Gaol, and their graves can be visited along the walkways – although records of where some are buried have now been lost over time.

One of the most famous was Elizabeth Woolcock who had the dubious honour of being the only female to have been executed in South Australia. She had been found guilty of poisoning her sick husband with mercury, and in 1873 was sentenced to hang – even though he was being treated by several different doctors, all of whom would probably have had small traces of mercury in their

Ghosts of the Past

(above)
The walkway where the graves of executed prisoners were buried. The graves were only given a burial number, initials and date of execution.

(left)
Flowers mark the location of Elizabeth Woolcock's grave. The marking above shows burial number '3', initials 'E.W.' and date '30.12.1873'.

medication! A 'retrial' was held recently and the same evidence presented, at which poor Elizabeth was found possibly not guilty. Ironically she had tried to commit suicide a year earlier by hanging herself, but the attempt failed. Some people feel she should not be buried here now, and still leave flowers on her grave.

The Early Days

But What of the Hauntings?

Ghostly stories had been coming out of the Gaol for many years prior to P.F.I. taking up the hunt. We had been given reports of staff working in the office on their own, who would hear footsteps crossing the upper floor when nobody was there and sounds of furniture moving around. Of another volunteer, who upon leaving the office to deal with the public in the shop, would return to find paperwork strewn across the floor, even after placing mugs of coffee on them. At one point, whatever it was, was told to "Stop!" as it was scaring this particular volunteer: it never happened again.

Then there were stories told of a lady dressed in white. In fact we were told of one school group which, after a sleepover, approached Sue Polkinghorne, one of our long-standing guides, the next day and asked where the mannequin had gone from one of the yards: it had been there the night before but was now missing. They were informed there had been no mannequin in that yard, but the teenagers insisted they had seen a lady dressed in white just standing there. The only lady on record who ever wore a white dress in the Gaol had been Elizabeth Woolcock at her execution. Could she still be haunting the place?

But the stories that interested us the most were the ones about the New Building where 21 of the hangings had taken place. It was regularly reported that a guard would be seen at the top of the old metal staircase. In fact records show that even when the Gaol was working, prisoners and guards alike often found it uncomfortable in this block and made requests to be moved. I interviewed a guard who used to work there and he informed me that a couple of the guards refused to do night duty in this block: they reported hearing somebody patrolling the gantries, when they themselves were sitting in their office.

Finally the Gaol was closed and the Adelaide City Council was called in to clear it out before it was opened to the public as a 'museum'. We tracked down a couple of the workers and found that after a few days they had felt uncomfortable about going back into the Gaol and to 'A' Wing in particular. They told of hearing footsteps, of doors slamming, and they were getting increasingly more alarmed.

And what about the electrician who, we were told, was up a step ladder adding some special lighting ready for a group who had hired the block for an upcoming celebration. If you can imagine yourself at the top of the stepladder and you glance through the bars, only to find a face smiling back at you through those

The New Building with 'C' wing on the left and 'B' wing on the right

bars… He ended up back at the office and told them "that if they want lights… they can… do it themselves!" He was determined he wasn't going back in there ever again either.

Then there was the work-experience student whose first job was to go into 'A' Wing and put up the new government 'No Smoking' signs. It wasn't long before he, too, ended up back at the office shaking. He said he had seen a guard in uniform come out of the top offices and run down one of the gantries and into a cell before disappearing. He was told that if he wanted to work there, he had to get used to the 'guard', as he was part of the Gaol.

And so the list of stories went on…

INTERVIEW WITH A FORMER GUARD

For those who claim the Gaol was only reported to be haunted AFTER it closed… the following is an interview done with one of the guards who worked there. We have talked to many, who have all told similar tales, but I have chosen to include this one in particular.

The Early Days

Some Background Information

A few years ago a local radio show went into the Adelaide Gaol for a night's stopover. Most of what took place was usual media stuff and nothing dramatic seemed to arise. However, one phone call came in that was of interest to us: it was from a gentleman who claimed to have been a guard stationed there between the years of 1986–88. He told the show of a paranormal experience he had when he was called to an area of the Gaol where a prisoner was thought to be escaping. The reason for this was because the figure of a man was being picked up on the security cameras. On arriving in the area it was found to be vacant with no prisoner to be seen. On double-checking back with security, they were quickly told that the figure was still being seen on the monitors and was directly in front of them.

For the years following this radio show, this had been nothing but a story as we had no way of verifying it. However, a year ago this very gentleman turned up on one of our tours at the Gaol and soon contacted me so that he could tell his story. The following interview includes Andrew's personal experience in the Gaol – and also tells of other well-known happenings amongst the guards who worked there with him.

Transcript of the Interview

Alison: *Thank you Andrew for contacting us and giving us some of your time for this interview.*
Andrew: *My pleasure.*
Alison: *Can you tell us a little about the Gaol, and in particular the 'paranormal' type experiences you have either heard about, or experienced yourself?*
Andrew: *When there were noises or smells and you were working, we would put it down to the criminals etc. as there were always smells e.g. boiler house, kitchen, maintenance… but the other night on the tour was quite remarkable. For instance, the bake house: while standing in Yard 6 there was the smell of freshly-baked bread; but when stepping away… nothing. And when we went down the laneway… again, freshly baked bread… not like a lingering smell, but like you had just walked past a bakery or something.*
Alison: *Did any of the others smell it?*
Andrew: *Oh yes, we ALL smelled it on the tour. I thought it was remarkable; but when we all moved off, it was gone.*
    And then in the New Building some of us were looking up the stairs for one reason or another, especially with the stories of the old guard being told etc, so we spent most of our time looking up there. I remember seeing this head up there

[points to the door in the office area off to the left] *because that was a canteen for the years I was here. The head looked out very quickly and went back in. I saw it quickly out of the corner of my eye; but I wasn't the only one, as there were three or four others that saw it exactly the same time, which I found interesting. I would have said male.*

I don't believe what is here is harmful... but I hear you had a nasty shove?

Alison: [Recounts a time I was at the foot of the stairs between the second and third cell when a violent shudder had passed through my body, forcing my head to crash back against the wall and chilling me to the bones. I have described on page 33.]

Andrew: *Well that third cell... we had a lot of problems with prisoners wanting to get out of there in the middle of the night.*

Alison: *Did they actually report saying why? What it was they saw or felt?*

Andrew: *I can't remember. But I do remember responding once myself to this, and we had to get the prisoner out. But the talk amongst ourselves was that the prisoner just wanted to get out, and we didn't actually interview him about it. For us to stop having to play Eight Balls somewhere, and then have to go move the prisoner out, was just a pain in the neck to us at the time. So it was a case of get them out... put them in another cell... and shut them up as quickly as possible: so we never stopped to ask them. The officers did talk about things amongst themselves, and they did talk about that cell and how they thought themselves there was something with that cell – especially as they had several people complain – so it makes you wonder doesn't it?*

Alison: *Did you ever hear anything in the Gaol, like people walking around?*

Andrew: *Well this staircase* [New Block] *and the rooms under it. The first door is where we would put our hats, lunches etc; also it was where the SCO* [Senior Correctional Officer] *used to sit. We would also sit in there during the first and second watch. There would always be an officer stationed there. But the problem about being in the New Building was the fact that so many people who worked there said it was so haunted – and anybody working here would have known that. In fact, it was so well known, that when they had a new officer on duty there, others would use the walkway outside and come up to the window and would stand at the window with a torch shining eerily up at their own face, and just stare in the window to scare the hell out of the new officer. We would always be doing stuff like that, particularly with the new officers.*

There was one new officer though... [name supplied] *who did a nightshift in the New Building, when he heard the noise of the Eight Balls moving on the pool table, and thought it was the patrol officers who may have come in for a game in between patrols. He thought nothing of it, and quickly finished the chapter of the book he had been reading and then went around the corner to have a look and to say hello: but when he came through the barrier and looked down, there was nothing there and no sound either. They discussed this amongst themselves, and put forward natural theories like: could the prisoners have taped it and replayed it (as they all had ghetto blasters etc)? But as the officer pointed out: yes, but it was just the balls; and no background noise. If the prisoner had done a tape – and because of the background noise that happens in a working Gaol – you should have heard other noises as well as the balls moving. But then, that very same night, he goes back to his book again when he can hear footsteps coming down the metal staircase. So he comes out of the office and looks through the barrier and through the staircase. He said he could still hear the footsteps but could see nobody on that staircase. And that was the last night that he ever worked in that New Building. He never wanted to work in it again.*

Alison: *It is good to hear they were being heard back then too!* [I then recount the story of these same footsteps passing Jeff and myself on the stairs, causing my body to react as if a static breeze had gone by.]

Gaol stairs in New Building

Ghosts of the Past

Andrew: *Another bloke, John…* [full name supplied] *worked New Building in 'A' Wing bottom. They used to have an officer's station on the right-hand side when coming in. The cell next to it was used as a storeroom for brooms, mops etc, as 'A' Wing was locked off to everywhere else and so had to have their own gear. John was in on one of the night watches. Control room staff had rung him and told him that one of the prisoners in a cell there was trying to speak to them; but the sound was muffled and they couldn't work out what he was saying. He goes into 'A' Wing… he sees the red light on outside the cell* [lights would come on so they knew which prisoner was trying to contact them], *but it slowly dawns on him that it was the storeroom cell – and nobody was in there. So he gets on the phone back to control and said it is a storeroom. They said they had it on the tapes, so he opens it up and switches off the red-light button. They said it was just a muffled faint voice that couldn't be made out. Every time the intercom system was accessed the tape would roll, and it would be recorded.*

And then there was this one night. I was on patrol, and John… [full name supplied] *was in the Control Room. Jock…* [full name supplied] *was on patrol with me. We went into Yard 2 and into the recreation room: guards often liked to get the stack of plastic plates and just throw them around, and then just walk out and leave them lying there, as it used to annoy the prisoners. Anyway, John gets us on the radio and says there's something between the walls, and to go and have a look as somebody is down there. I don't know why we walked a different way round, but this time we went past the Hanging Tower to Section 4 corner. So we came around the corner but can't see anybody. John was shouting to us: "Right in front of you, right in front of you!" and we both just stood there and radioed back "No, there's nobody here". We were feeling uncomfortable standing there though. We headed out of there and back to the stairs to the Control Room, which nobody ever liked, mainly because they always felt unsafe.* [Control room was up the small stairs and into the old Governor's Quarters]. *When up there John says: "Look!" and on playing the tape back there was a form…* [described as more solid than a misty form]. *My first thought was 'Yeah alright… there must be something wrong with the tape' mainly because these tapes of course were reused. They used to have seven tapes, Monday to Sunday, and the cameras used to run on 1-frame-every-20-seconds unless something happens; and then you would hit record-at-normal-speed. I believe this tape never got recycled as it had something unusual on it – but I don't know. I wasn't doing anything on last day at the Gaol and everything got boxed.*

Three months later I was watching this thing on a supermarket in America. Groceries would be thrown off the shelf, so they put up security cameras. They called some 'ghostbusters' in. I was watching this, and they put their own video cameras up and they explained why. They flooded it with infra-red lighting.

The interesting thing is that all the big cameras with big boxes in the Gaol had two big lights... and they were infra-red lights which made the night seem like day. I started to wonder if this had something to do with it as the Gaol cameras worked with infra-red. The question is: was the tape knackered? But you have to remember that they saw it on the monitor at the time – not just the tape.

Alison: [Questions on the possibility that it could be insects on the lens of the camera? This causes a misty-type image moving around and can look humanised etc.]

Andrew: *No, it just looked like somebody standing there and it didn't move around.*

Alison: *Would you know what would be on the tape label if it was kept?*

Andrew: *Not sure if they would have kept it. They would keep incidents, e.g. riots, drug drops etc., and they would keep those as part of evidence. It would be taken off the tapes and would be put on a master tape. A ghost sighting would not be seen as an incident that would be called up at a later date for court, so may not be put on master tape. But it would be on a master tape if it exists still.*

Alison: *An ex-prisoner once told me that the bottom end cell of Yard 4 was used as a library and the prisoners complained about the books being thrown around at night. Could this just be an example of the guards messing around?*

Andrew: *Could have been: but if it was the guards he would have heard them approaching, as guards couldn't go anywhere without them being heard due to the footwear and the keys rattling.*

With that we move on to general chatting and the interview finishes.

Ghosts of the Past

Cell Block 'D' in Yard 4

Chapter 2
The Hunt Begins

"I could hear old-style piano music coming from the cellblock in Yard 2 near the cells with the Elizabeth Woolcock dummy. It seemed to be drifting through from the yard behind."
(Jennifer, Ghost Tour)

DO YOU think the Adelaide Gaol would let us in to investigate? I asked Jeff one day. Like most new teams, finding places to investigate had been a major hurdle. 'Cemetery hopping' had been the main focus, although we did also have our team member's house when we needed to do indoor work. This was great for trying out new ideas and perfecting techniques, but now we were chomping at the bit to find something we could really get our teeth into. We really needed somewhere to be able to put these new techniques into practice, and what better place than a 170-year-old historic building rumoured to be haunted.

Jeff had visited the Gaol to discuss with management the possibility of us coming in over a period of time to conduct investigations and see if we could back up those rumours and stories with some concrete evidence. Around three to six months should do it, we thought, after that we would move on to other places.

—ooo—

"We have it!" Jeff stated triumphantly.

"Yes!!!" I grinned, almost doing a little dance of joy on the spot. At last we had a project of magnitude that we could really put our efforts into. "When do we start?" I asked eagerly. "Tomorrow would be good for me!" I grinned.

As it happened our investigations started soon after. At first it was only when there was a volunteer caretaker able to stay to oversee that we behaved in the appropriate manner. After all, the Manager really knew very little about us, and was wary after having had bad experiences with 'ghost hunters' previously. Over the months though, a working relationship and a trust was formed and we were allowed in more regularly, as long as it didn't interfere with tours or functions, which was fine with us as this would have tainted evidence anyway.

And so it was that on 20th November 2002, Paranormal Field Investigators arrived at the Gaol for their very first investigation. Little did we know then that we would be there for a further eight years and beyond!

—o0o—

So there we were at last, an eager team of investigators who had been waiting patiently for this night to arrive and the enthusiasm certainly was not lacking. The conditions appeared right for this November evening, with the weather being kind by giving us fine and mild conditions.

"Look it is a full moon too," one of the investigators added excitedly. At this early stage of our work, like many others, we felt a full moon would help with the possible activity we may experience in the Gaol. After all, all good Hollywood horror movies always included a full moon! Over the many years to come, and with careful data keeping, we soon noted that better results seemed to be achieved at the opposite end of the moon cycle. Still, these were early days, and over the years our ideas and techniques evolved, from data collection to theories changing.

We stood momentarily and looked around at the daunting size of the area we would have to cover during the course of the night. Set on approximately nine acres, the Gaol consisted of six yards, two towers, and eleven main building areas. Now all we had to work out was the not-so-simple task on how best to cover this with just seven people and only three hours to do it in. Having already briefed the team on how we would best start, we broke up and set about taking baseline readings mainly from the buildings we knew we would be covering that night. This way, if there were any changes such as in temperature or Electro Magnetic Fields (EMF), we would have some guidelines to fall back on.

For those that are new to the word EMF I will give a brief explanation here before moving on.

It is theorised by some that changes in the Electro Magnetic Fields, which are all around us, could indicate a possible paranormal presence. A meter referred to as a gauss meter detects such fluctuations in the electromagnetic fields, with your average EMF Meter only doing so in the AC/DC fields. A more expensive

Trifield Meter is far more preferable due to taking three axis measurements at once and covering a larger spectrum. The average gauss meter is also only calibrated 50/60HZ (which is what your electrics run at) and offers scales 0-5 mG and 0-50 mG. Therefore it would only be an assumption that if paranormal phenomena existed that it would work in this small range of the field. It is interesting to note that anything over 2 mG is considered unhealthy and tests have shown that it can affect the human brain, giving effects similar to a 'haunting'.

It was whilst doing these baselines of the New Building it was noted that one of the cells seemed to read much colder on the temperature meter than any of the previous cells tested.

"Perhaps it is just a draught causing it," suggested Alan as he peered through the opening into Cell #65. Always the rational one, he was quick to look for natural explanations for most things. He quizzically looked back down at the reading he had just taken from within the cell… a good 9-10 degrees cooler than any of the other cells he had previously tested: in fact cooler than the outside temperature. He tested the handle hoping the door would open easily, but was disappointed to find it immoveable. He shrugged and moved on. After all, without access to the cell, there was nothing further to be done there.

Thirty minutes later the New Building was covered. Baseline readings had been achieved and monitoring equipment set in place. Now all that remained was to split into teams of two and position ourselves around this silent, double storey, T-shaped cell block.

"I think I just saw something," Colin looked harder into the gloom that lay up on the second floor gantry. "I thought I just saw a shadow moving, like a person or animal up there," he said pointing up to the vicinity of Cell #65, "It could just have been imagination though," he added quickly.

Although chills were felt on occasion for the next hour, nothing definite was experienced and so it was that Jeff and Bill decided to change their positions and wandered down the gantry to recheck the temperature of Cell #65. It was at this point there was a sudden turn of events.

Bill reacted to something. "Are you OK?" Jeff asked curiously, as he tried to keep this possible new turn of events within the sights of the video camera he was carrying as he followed from behind. Bill didn't have time to reply before Jeff's camera started to crash towards the ground, the final descent fortunately being stopped by the strap still attached around his neck. Jeff gasped loudly as an icy feel had suddenly hit him full on. "It was like a bucket of ice had been thrown over me," he later described the feeling to the team. "All the hair on my body reacted by rising up," he added. Whether it was a reaction to the sheer cold or to the unseen force, he couldn't determine.

"I felt the same cold," Bill concurred when adding his story. "Something grabbed my arm as I wandered past Cell #65, but it felt so icy, much like Jeff described."

Both men had been taken by surprise: they had expected sounds, and had hoped to witness something – but neither had expected the shock of this sensation as if touched by something cold and chilling. It took them a few moments to get their breathes back and to regain their composure enough to continue the investigation in that area. Bill kept grumbling that it was still cold there, especially around his legs, so Jeff concentrated the video on the area indicated. The camera did show a moving spherical object, but due to the amount of insects and dirt in the cell block at the time it cannot be discounted that this was purely coincidence and was just this. It was a full fifteen minutes before Bill and Jeff had relief from that icy feel; as if it was taking time for the body to finally thaw out.

—000—

Round the corner in 'A' Wing things were becoming curious there too. Another member, who also coincidentally shared my name, had walked through the darkened area, pausing on reaching the end of the block to rub at the back of her neck and forehead. It was strange how quickly the headache had come on. No warning, just a sudden pain in the head which she described later as almost a twitching pain. Mel, our guest who had been standing outside and on noticing that Alison was not now behind her, rejoined her inside. It was at that point Mel too stopped momentarily: she felt a sudden pain which struck on the left side of her head. She stepped back in surprise, only to find the pain quickly subsided and was replaced with welcome relief.

"Well, you were standing under the trapdoor of the gallows," Jeff mentioned to them later as they discussed this strange experience. They had been totally unaware at the time that the area they were standing in was where twenty-one people lost their lives. Coincidence? Psychosomatic? Or were they feeling emotions and pain felt long ago? One can only wonder.

—000—

The Hunt Begins

Cell Block 'D' where the light appeared (top floor far end)

"We only have around 40 minutes left," I glanced at my watch in disbelief on how quickly the time had flown. "Maybe you guys should try at least one other area before we wrap it up for the night."

Bill nodded and agreed that it was probably a good idea, "We could maybe wander down to Yard 4 and check out that cell block there". He had been meaning to go and visit the cell after hearing the stories told of the light coming on, and of the door re-opening by itself. If they were quick, they could spend some time there photographing and making notes for our hopeful return visit. Jeff decided to accompany him, as he too was curious about the stories told from up there.

"Did we leave a light on up there?" Bill pointed at the light that was now shining brightly out of the top end cell of Cell Block 'D'. Jeff shook his head, explaining that they couldn't be sure that it wasn't one of the volunteers earlier in the day. "But didn't we come through here earlier?" Bill added, "Surely we would have noticed it then". After all, he reasoned, the style of the cell block in this yard was different to the New Building. Unlike the more modern cells which opened internally within the building, these older cells opened out externally to yards. For this reason any lights that had been switched on should have been more easily noticed when entering the yards at any time.

"Well… let's go check it out," Bill said, already bounding towards the stone stairs that led up to the second storey.

Upon reaching the cell, both men peered into the open door and viewed the room, which was empty apart from a single bed that stood on its own. As they wandered in for a closer look, there seemed nothing amiss; no air of gloom or strangeness was evident. A few photographs were taken before they decided to move on elsewhere. Walking back, past the silent cells with their locked doors, they discussed where they would head next. A sudden and violent sound caused both men to jump. The large grille on the cell door they had just passed began to rattle furiously, causing them both to spin back around. To their amazement the door of the last cell had reopened. Going back to test the door, they could see nothing obvious; but they both made a note that the door was extremely heavy – not one prone to movement in such a light breeze.

"Whatever it was seems to have gone," Jeff surmised as they stood waiting for further signs of activity. By then all was quiet. "I guess we should wrap up the investigation for tonight." Jeff pulled his two-way from his pocket and radioed back to the New Building to see if I was also ready to wrap it up. It was agreed, and the night ended there.

—000—

The next investigation was soon upon us only a week later. Our first point of call, naturally, was to investigate Cell #65 a little more so we could try and work out why this particular cell had proved to be so cold on our last investigation. Once the cell had been unlocked giving us unrestricted access, we soon discovered the cause. The cell now read normal and was in keeping with the temperature from the other cells. The fault had been with the way the temperature had been taken. Working with a thermometer designed to take surface temperature, Patrick had struggled to aim it through the peephole of the locked door. It appeared that it had hit the window of the cell which, when tested this night, did read the same 10.5 degrees that it was producing the week before. Mystery solved!

Infra Red laser thermometers are regularly used by paranormal teams around the world. However these were designed to take surface temperatures, not ambient air temperature, and are specialised for the food/motor industry. For this reason when used incorrectly the thermometer can give a false reading in the minus degrees. P.F.I. now only use this instrument to verify cold areas on our body, e.g. if we feel cold on one cheek as if touched.

The mystery that wasn't solved, however, was the effect the gallows of the New Building seemed to be having on various members of the team. Tonight was no different. It was quickly noticed upon entering this area, that the atmosphere was much changed from the first time we had been there. It wasn't described as oppressive: just plain 'creepy'.

Jeff was the first to feel the effects of the area. Standing on the top floor of 'A' Wing near the gallows, he gasped as a pain seized the back of his head. He quickly moved away from the area and returned to the stairs. By the time he reached the foot of the stairs the pain had subsided. On joining the investigator who was operating the camera below that area, he was greeted with the information that the camera, whilst recording, had just switched itself off.

"My hair was rising up," the investigator stated, "just like there was a build up of static around me".

All was checked: the battery was fine and the tape running smoothly. It could just have been a glitch in the camera – or could it be that something just didn't want us to video tape at that point?

Meanwhile, another team member was having his own experience in a separate part of the Gaol.

"Bill, are you OK?" I looked with concern at the man who was now standing in front of me half smiling. The smile that lay on his face did not appear to be one of joy; but instead, one of disbelief.

"I will be in a minute," said Bill as he slowly sat down and reached for the coffee that I had now placed in front of him. Taking a sip, he continued to tell of what had just happened. Apparently he had wandered down to that problematic cell in Yard 4 with the intention of sitting quietly, meditating and seeing what would happen. He had closed the door behind himself and settled on the bed that still remained in the cell. Sitting there, he had waited for his eyes to adjust to the darkness before continuing. It was as he sat there that he felt it… the mattress sinking next to him. "It was as if somebody had sat down with me," he said shaking his head, "it was very definite and did NOT give a good feel at all!" With that he took another sip of coffee as other team members left for a quick inspection of the cell. But, as normally happens, there was now nothing to be seen or felt.

—000—

"Alright, let's go over what we found that night". It was meeting night, and I joined the rest of the team at Patrick's table, coffee in hand. "Did anybody capture anything of note?"

"Well, we did get plenty of photographs of light anomalies," Jeff said excitedly. Bill nodded his head and started to explain that he too had taken numerous photographs that seemed to show many spheres of light moving around. This was 2002 and the subject of 'orbs' was becoming popular amongst groups at this time. "In fact I have so many in some of my photos, I have just dubbed them the 'Party Shots'," he laughed. We were all eager to view these and, anticipating this, Bill handed us all CDs with the photos on them for us to view later.

Orbs are spherical balls of light that appear commonly in digital photographs, especially when taken with a flash. They are extremely controversial: some hold on to a belief that they are 'spirit lights', whilst others believe the more natural explanation that these anomalies are nothing more then dust, moisture, pollen etc. close to the lens and caught in the flash. Having done extensive experiments ourselves with our own cameras, P.F.I. are inclined to largely agree with the natural theory.

By far the most interesting thing we caught that night, however, was potentially our very first Electronic Voice Phenomena (EVP) recording. All around the world, investigation teams appear to capture voices on recording equipment. These are voices that the investigators themselves didn't hear at the time. Like any other type of 'paranormal evidence', there is a lot of controversy surrounding EVP. Theories range from voices of the dead being manipulated onto the tapes, or stray radio signals; right through to simple audio pareidolia, where the brain will try and make sense of random noise and interpret something as a voice – much like we do visually with faces in clouds and other mundane items. P.F.I. do try to be careful with this type of data. We always use new tapes and always have back-up video to show it wasn't one of our team members whispering or moving. The reason for this? Movement of clothing can still produce a very nice EVP! Stomach rumbling can too! It is because of this problem that any natural noise is announced by us on the recordings at the time too.

Being our first time in the Gaol, we were… to put it mildly… slightly disorganised. We had noisily set up the equipment, laughing and joking as we did so, before deciding to step out for a while to discuss further tactics. A voice recorder had been running the whole time, and it was as we left and the door is heard closing behind us, that a loud audible sigh is heard on the tape recorder… almost as if it was a "Thank God they are gone!"

The Hunt Begins

It was a small snippet of maybe something from the whole night, but it was enough to keep us eager to go back and take a second look at the Gaol.

"Well we certainly had enough happen that it would be worth our time going back," I surmised. "If we say around a six-month's investigation there, we should have some indication by then if it is truly haunted or not".

Little did we know we would still be there eight years later – and for some of us, still there to this day!

Ghosts of the Past

The Hanging Tower

Chapter 3
Let the Show Go On

"Upon entering the Hanging Tower, I had a tightness of the chest and a feeling of sickness. I nearly passed out and a feeling of wanting to cry swept over me."

(Christine, Ghost Tour)

IT'S GOOD to be back at last, I smiled as I stepped over the threshold of the Gaol. It seemed too long since we last had been there.

It had been approximately six weeks since our last investigation of the Gaol. The P.F.I. break over Christmas and the New Year period had been extended due to other commitments, and this January night was the first night the team had been able to assemble. It was a night that was proving uncomfortable for us all – but more for climatic reasons rather then paranormal.

"35 degrees!" I stated, as I wiped away the beads of sweat that were starting to form on my brow, and frowned at the temperature meter. The sun was sinking behind the orange-glowing walls, yet still the Gaol was retaining its hot daytime temperature. "Well at least if we feel a cold spot tonight, we are going to know it is for real!"

Tonight was also a little different as we had brought three guests with us, one of them being Darren. Darren had contacted us during our hiatus to see if we would be interested in making a short documentary as he worked for a local current affair show and had a personal interest in the paranormal. To get a feel for what was on offer, he requested to be able to come along on an investigation at the Gaol with us; a request that was granted. Also invited were a clairvoyant and her partner to assist on this investigation and see if any new information could be uncovered that could be verified.

Whether it was the hot conditions or just a quiet night in general, possible paranormal activity seemed lacking on this occasion. Apart from a $-4°C$ reading in Yard 4 by Bill with the laser pointed thermometer, nothing appeared that could be classed out of the ordinary which was disappointing for Darren. Like many who visit the Gaol for the first time, Darren had arrived expecting to see full-bodied apparitions and we had to explain that the paranormal phenomena doesn't quite work like that. In fact, if it was this regular, and we could promise this every time, there would be no need to investigate the subject as everybody would be witnessing it. Even better, the Gaol would become a Mecca for believers and none-believers alike... all camped out in the car park. I personally wish it WAS that easy, it would certainly make my tours a lot easier to take!

We did have one incident with Bill that night. He had stationed himself in the marquee that had been permanently erected in the yard behind the New Building.

"My hand..." he suddenly said, "there is a strange sensation on it". Instead of retracting it, he stretched it out further, feeling to see if there was a definite spot that was making his hand feel like this. The other investigators stationed with him started to gather around peering into the empty space that Bill was now feeling around in.

"Bill, there is a man of authority standing right in front of you," the clairvoyant began, "he is testing you!" She dropped her head down and went momentarily silent whilst she tried to pick up more. "I can't tell if he is an inmate or an officer... but he is in charge... and, wait... there are more of them". She looked back up and glanced around the marquee, "The room is full of lights and the authoritative spirit has called them in".

Clairvoyance is hard to scientifically verify. For this reason and because P.F.I. was more involved in getting hard physical evidence for the paranormal, we moved away from using clairvoyants. This does not mean that we do not agree with clairvoyants, and we do sometimes recommend cases to clairvoyants if this is the area the clients are more interested in. For this reason though, sadly none of the information that the clairvoyant gave to Bill could be verified. Nor could the information that followed regarding the spirit of a young girl dressed in white who approached the clairvoyant, having recognised her from when she had visited previously on a Ghost Tour.

"She is showing me that she likes to play the piano," the clairvoyant said. This was interesting as it was only later that we found out that piano playing had indeed been heard several times in the Gaol – and was to be heard in a future investigation by two of our own investigators! She moved closer to the original 1841 cells and clutched her stomach: "There is also a large, obese man here, who had a senior role here in the Gaol." She went on to explain that he was giving her a feeling of sickness. Could it have been Governor Ashton, the first Governor of the Adelaide Gaol? After all it was reported that he did weigh in at approximately 146 kg. It is rumoured that he too has remained in the Gaol and can be heard walking around the upper floors of the Governor's House.

But as with most information given in clairvoyance form it is hard to verify and, as such, is considered to be inconclusive. Over the years that the Gaol was working, there were many people who worked there and who would also have had family members living both inside and outside the walls. Records were not kept or have been lost on many of these individuals.

"Well, sorry you didn't get to experience too much tonight," I placed my equipment in the boot of the car carefully and turned back to Darren. "Sadly it seems to have been one of those quiet nights here". Darren shrugged: "It just makes me want to come back more," he laughed, "Besides, there was that incident tonight where my camera malfunctioned". He went on to explain to me how he had been in the New Building videotaping when his battery suddenly showed empty: "The camera then just switched off… Thing is, it came back on moments later and showed the battery was fully charged again."

I smiled and nodded my head… this was going to be a story I would hear many times and experience myself in future years to come.

—000—

I stood up and pushed back a strand of damp hair off my face. It was now a month later and the Current Affair show had arrived to do the filming. Jeff and I had decided that because of the dust question-mark with 'orbs', we would diligently mop and clean the whole of the New Building. Quite a task, considering it is in three large sections and double storey! We decided though, this was better than to wash down each of the ninety-two cells, keeping the doors shut seemed to be the better option.

Having finished my sections, I wandered down the stairs and paused, deciding I had better let Jeff know I was leaving. Momentarily I lowered my bucket on the ground and leant across the metal banister of the staircase, straining my neck up to try and locate where Jeff was.

The New Building, 'B' wing is on the left and 'A' wing on the right

"I'm heading back," I called up to him. A muffled acknowledgement was heard in response.

It was then that I froze: the cell door I was standing next to slowly – but surely – opened to well over 45 degrees in front of me. 'Just a breeze,' I thought reassuringly to myself. The reassurance only lasted momentarily though, until I remembered just why I had damp hair and a T-shirt that was now sticking to me: it had been an extremely warm day with no air movement. Being worse in this old stone building, cleaning had been extremely uncomfortable and I wasn't sorry to see the back of it. A breeze today would have been a welcome event.

I quickly set the bucket back down and wandered into the cell. It didn't feel any different; no expected chill, and no feel of a breeze on my raised hand, especially close to the small window that lay on the far side of the room. 'Maybe just a freak wind,' I decided. The coffee I was longing for was calling more strongly, so picking up my bucket I headed back to the dormitories where we were stationed.

Shortly after, Jeff paused to listen to the creaking of what sounded like a cell door opening. He had now moved closer to the staircase with his cleaning and was relieved that he was nearly finished. Having also completed the spraying of the insect spray to cut down this factor, he headed down the stairs.

"Alison, is that you?" he called out, expecting to hear my voice in answer. He was greeted with only silence. He wandered down the stairs to find the left-hand cell at the bottom was now wide open. 'Strange,' he thought, as we had ensured all the doors were shut earlier.

Back at the dormitories, he asked me if I had opened the cell. "No, it actually opened in front of me too, and I closed it again before I left". I pointed at our equipment still packed safely away and added, "It's always the way isn't it; something happens and all you have in your hands is a mop and bucket". This was going to prove truer as the night went on: this door had not finished with us just yet!

Problem cell door at foot of stairs

Ghosts of the Past

And so the filming began. Cameras rolled, and endless scenes were re-taken from every conceivable angle; and for us, standing around waiting for what they needed next was more tiring then actually doing any investigation work. Anybody who has worked with the media would agree that it isn't quite as glamorous as it would appear. After having done more media events, I will take my hat off to those who do it for a living. Although having a love of photography and video editing myself, I have always found behind the camera far more interesting work than in front of it.

Earlier in the evening the team and the guest clairvoyants had met for tea, to go over the plan of action for the night once we arrived at the Gaol. Knowing how sensational the media can make this subject matter, we knew we had to be careful. This seemed like a good opportunity to sit and cover how this could be done successfully. Although Darren had seemed genuine in his quest for the story, we knew that at the end of the day the editing would probably be out of his hands. We also decided that no real investigation could be undertaken until the show had left the Gaol, which they planned to do in the early hours of the morning. It was then that we would stay back and do the real work.

One added advantage of having the TV camera crew in filming, was that we were able to make use of their own miniature cameras, one of which worked in infra-red, a light spectrum that is invisible to the human eye, but not to these cameras. It was decided the New Building would be the focus for these: one upstairs in 'A' Wing looking down towards the mannequins at the end, and the other would be trying to capture the cell door performing its opening-and-closing manoeuvre that Jeff and myself had been witnessing earlier that afternoon. If it opened this time, we would have it on video… one problem though: the camera only worked with lights on – a problem that would be a real issue later that evening. As the camera rolled, the door typically remained completely still and silent.

"I can sense a man down here," one of the clairvoyants clutched her chest, eyes closed, and raised her hand. Standing down by the main door of 'B' Wing the other two clairvoyants huddled around her, agreeing that they too could feel this man's energy. Although the information presented was vague, we decided to film our own footage of the proceedings and made the decision to turn off the lights to enable us do so in the infra-red mode. This also meant that the TV crew's own camera would now not be able to see. The light was off for two minutes only before we wandered back up to turn them on… to find that in those two minutes the cell door had opened, only this time silently enough that nobody had heard it.

There it stood, wide open, taunting us that the cameras had missed this event. Yet again a case of 'if your cameras are rolling' forget it… the moment you turn them off or point away… well now you can understand our frustrations!

Another example of this frustration for the night would be the Hanging Tower. Having set up two cameras in there, mine was aimed from the back cells out towards the main door. However, it was just off the door on the wall to one side. Having set up the cameras we left, closing and engaging the large sliding bolt on the entrance door as we did. On returning twenty minutes later to retrieve the cameras, we found that the door was now open to just over 20 degrees. Strange, since not only was the door a heavy door, but the sliding bolt isn't the easiest to pull back. All investigators were accounted for – so it certainly wasn't us – and the film crew had left half-an-hour earlier.

"Hopefully we will have caught whatever it was on tape," I smiled enthusiastically, unscrewing my camera off the tripod. My smile soon turned to frustration on looking back over the footage. It is clear at what point the door opened as the light on the wall increases… was it a supernatural or a real person playing a trick? We will never know. Leading up to and at the point the door opens, a freight train passes by the Gaol and any sound of somebody walking up the metal walkway or drawing back the bolt is drowned out at that moment. Again we were left with nothing but questions and frustrations. It would be years later that a teenager on one of the Ghost Tours asked me: "How do you think they view you?" alluding to the 'ghosts'. I paused contemplating this question, "I think if there are ghosts here, they see us as their entertainment," I laughed.

As the night wore on it was beginning to seem that now the film crew had left, after an uneventful night, the place had come alive.

It was getting to the end of what had been a long night, and I for one was ready to go home and get some sleep. The sun would be coming up in another hour or so, and I had been packing up my own equipment into the cases left at the foot of the stairs in 'B' Wing. Finishing, I had stood up and started chatting to Megan who had been standing near the opposite wall to where I now stood. Suddenly a violent shudder passed through my body causing my head to slam back hard against the wall. We have all had that 'somebody-has-just-walked-over-my-grave' shudder, which is a normal body reaction – not paranormal. This, however, would have been approximately fifteen times more violent, and simultaneously the body chilled and the bones felt like they had just turned to ice. It was moments before I could speak; the shock had been that great. Quickly I staggered to the stairs and slowly sank down to sit on one, shaking and rubbing at my arms, trying to regain some warmth.

"Are you OK?" Megan asked me curiously after hearing my loud gasp. I found myself unable to answer Megan at that very moment due to the pain in my skull, and I furiously rubbed the back of my head.

"Oh my God, I don't know what that was," I looked up at Megan who was still observing me curiously. Now that I had at least regained my breath, I explained what had just happened. "I feel like I am unclean, and I need a shower," I continued. I waited for the chill to pass, but it would be a further twenty minutes before the relief finally crept in.

Could it have been a condition of the brain? Possibly, but I have never suffered from such a condition before, and have never experienced anything like it since. For a long time on the Ghost Tours we were to take in the future, I never spoke of this incident. After all, it was personal to me and how would I back it up? However this changed recently as more people have experienced the same feeling standing at the same spot. Twice I have had to calm down shaking people who have complained of having their shoulders slammed back against the wall before half their body turned to ice.

It is at this point I will remind people of the interview with Andrew regarding his experiences as a guard in the working years of the Gaol. I will repeat an excerpt here:

Andrew: *Well that third cell is where we had a lot of problems with prisoners wanting to get out of there in the middle of the night.*

Alison: *Did they actually report saying they saw anything or felt anything?*

Andrew: *I can't remember, but I do remember responding once myself to this, and we had to get the prisoner out. But the talk amongst ourselves was that the prisoners were just wanting to get out, and we didn't actually interview them about it. For us to actually stop having to play Eight Balls somewhere, and then have to go move the prisoner out, was just a pain in the neck to us at the time. So it was a case of get them out, put them in another cell and shut them up as quickly as possible: so we never stopped to ask them. The officers did talk about things amongst themselves, and they did talk about that cell and how they thought themselves there was something up with that cell, as they had had several people complain, so it makes you wonder doesn't it?*

Let the Show Go On

Cell 3 is the cell next to the one that had been opening all night. I had been standing directly between the two cells when I had my experience. Coincidence? Maybe… the world is indeed full of them!

—oOo—

Over the following weeks we started to go through our material taken from the night. Sadly – or maybe fortunately – the TV show had cancelled the short documentary, and the driving force behind it, Darren, moved on interstate to another job.

"Is that dust?" I pointed to the screen. Quickly we rewound the tape a short way and viewed again a section of footage taken by one of the small stationary cameras overlooking the hanging area in 'A' Wing. A small pulsating ball of light appeared from the side of the camera and seemed to go under one of the cross beams, over another, and then travelled down to the other end of the block where it hovered momentarily over the clairvoyants who were standing below it near

At the foot of the stairs in 'B' Wing

the hanging beam. It then moved down and appeared to disappear behind the mannequins, reappearing moments later out the other side. This is probably our most controversial footage – even for us. We have long believed orbs to be dust and other environmental factors, and still do: yet here was one that seemingly travelled away from the camera and moved behind objects at a distance. Common sense told us that it was just a trick of the lens; but still the question remains as to whether this is such a simple answer. We have viewed it frame by frame hoping to debunk it like we have a lot of our other footage and photos. Still it appears to travel under bars and behind objects. As technology advances, so does the software: so hopefully in time we will be able to get an answer one way or another.

The following photos are fairly pixelated and grainy due to fact they were taken from security camera footage. To be printed they also need to be lightened up. Hopefully you still get an idea of what I am trying to explain.

There was also one last surprise from this night; but it wasn't found until months later. Whilst reviewing his videotape to write up a report, Jeff stumbled upon P.F.I.'s second Electronic Voice Phenomena from the Gaol. Jeff found what appeared to be a voice on the tape that had been neither his nor Megan's – the only two people to have remained in the New Building after everybody else had left. A male voice clearly whispers, what appears to be a name. The surname of 'Murphy' is very audible, and is our interpretation of what we are hearing. What sounds like 'Sergeant' seems to precede it. It should be remembered that this is a large, empty stone building. When talking, voices echo, and listening to Jeff and Megan this is indeed true. The name whispered loudly, however, does not echo as if embedded onto the tape. It should also be noted that P.F.I. always use sealed tapes at all times, to avoid leeching from past recordings.

Who was Sergeant Murphy? Sadly we may never know. Many guards and people passed through this Gaol over her 147 years of service. Murphy would have been a common name due to the large Irish population that emigrated here. Was it the guard giving us his name, or his name being spoken by somebody else? Sadly, all we are left with once more is just another mystery.

Let the Show Go On

Photo 1 shows the 'orb' moving away from camera.

Photo 2 shows the 'orb' approaching the bars.

Photo 3 shows the 'orb' apparently disappearing behind the bars.

Photo 4 shows the 'orb' reappearing from behind the bars.

Ghosts of the Past

The Hanging Tower

Chapter 4
A Night to Remember

"Upon entering the Remand Centre, I felt goose bumps. I also felt heavy and sick and found it difficult to go in there. Most definitely not a good area."

(Melanie, Ghost Tour)

DO YOU feel that? I glanced nervously at the team who had just stepped over the threshold with me, and into the Old Adelaide Gaol's dark interior.

Tonight the atmosphere was different; it felt moody, oppressive and had a certain unwelcoming feel. The team shivered, but not because of the cold June winter's night, it was that they too were feeling the uneasiness wrapping itself round them. In previous months of investigation on these premises we had never felt quite so uncomfortable, and at this point we were almost reluctant to move forward… almost… for we reminded ourselves that this is exactly why we were here. Moving forward into areas that felt uneasy came with practice; and practice we had plenty of. Still, nothing would prepare us for the June night ahead that we were about to face.

"So how are we going to do this?" I asked Jeff.

Summer had passed by and Winter had descended rapidly and, although we had conducted a couple of other investigations in between, there had been nothing monumental to report to the Manager. It had been fairly quiet on that front. Which is why we were surprised to find it feeling so different this night.

Our last two investigations had produced only a small amount of curious happenings. One of these had occurred with one of our guests. She had been sitting at the top of the stairs in the New Building when she heard a female voice say "I will meet you at the…" the voice then faded away before the sentence could be completed. She became unnerved as she knew that I was the only other female investigator there that night, and I was far away in the Hanging Tower at this point in time. Suddenly she felt freezing cold and a pain struck the right side of her face accompanied by a tingling sensation in her cheek that lasted for a few minutes before finally wearing off.

As years went by, we were to come across accounts of this possible female presence in the New Building again – which was strange as there had never been any female prisoners kept in this section of the Gaol. The figure of a lady dressed in grey has been witnessed several times, often just behind the old black iron staircase. In fact in later years a girl approached me and told of how she had been helping with the catering for a function one night and had been stationed in the New Building. It was at the end of the night that she had noticed movement out of her peripheral vision. Thinking it was a guest who hadn't gone home yet, she walked out of what was once the guards' office, only to be stopped in her tracks. As she stood there in disbelief, she found herself looking at the figure of a lady dressed in an old-style grey dress who walked passed her before disappearing. Stories continue to surface of this apparition; but who was this 'Lady in Grey'? We may never know her identity; but we may later have found clues as to how she possibly came to be there.

But for now, here we stood: 28th June 2003. It was a night that would be remembered by us all and talked about for many years to come.

—000—

"Sorry guys, the crew got called out to do another project at the last minute," Darren from the Current Affair show had arrived. "I couldn't resist joining in though myself," he added eagerly.

The paranormal had been an interest of his for many years, and this was a great opportunity for him to get his hands dirty in the field and hopefully experience something for himself.

"Wow," he faltered as he too stepped through the door and looked around apprehensively, "this feels very different tonight," he shuddered. We just nodded our agreement and proceeded up to the Dormitories, our chosen base for the night.

"I am just going for a wander and a smoke," Bill said as he stood up and stretched. He looked around at the rest of the team who were all still chatting and finishing up the last of their meal. Picking up his camera he strolled out of the Dormitory. His wanderings soon took him to the Remand Centre's rear door. Deciding to take advantage of the dark interior he stepped through and settled himself under the painting of an Aboriginal gentleman, a memory left by a prisoner from long ago who had painted it on the end wall. He listened to nothing but silence and thought to himself how eerie it felt in there tonight. Although he had no plans as he entered, he now decided that he would try a spot of meditation and see if this made any difference. His camera, sitting obediently at his side, would be waiting at the ready in case it did.

The minutes ticked away as Bill journeyed off into his own world of relaxation. The tranquil feel that was washing over him proved to be short lived, however, as a noise from above him slammed him back into reality, his senses becoming alert once more. Was that snoring he had just heard? Yes, there it was again. Definite snoring and movements coming from the floor above, as if somebody was having a restless night's sleep. He knew this was impossible; after all the gate to the upper level of this cellblock was locked and for good reason, as the floor above had been

Remand Centre looking down towards the back door. The painting of the bearded aboriginal head can be seen on the end wall.

Ghosts of the Past

Remand Centre second floor.

deemed unsafe. More sounds… this time from down towards the museum area… movement… he knew this couldn't be possible. The team had been left behind in the Dormitory; and besides, any entry into the Remand from the museum end would result in the sensor light triggering, something which clearly hadn't happened. The atmosphere around him had just become thicker, and now a strong feeling of panic was starting to rise. Bill was experienced enough, however, not to let this overtake him: he knew to stand his ground. It was then he saw it, the dark figure of a man. Not quite a shadow, yet not quite solid. The figure flitted quickly across the arched doorway that separated the museum from the cell block. The dull green glow cast from the Exit sign highlighted the figure as it approached the locked gate leading to the stairs before finally disappearing through. NOW seemed like an ideal time to go and get some much needed backup!

I glanced up as Bill hurried back in to join the team. I could tell something was very wrong even from a distance. Normally calm and poised, Bill's gait was hurried and his face anxious.

"You OK?" I asked as he joined us at the table.

A Night to Remember

"Once I stop shaking, I will be," he said before taking a deep breath and excitedly relaying to us what had just happened.

"Looks like it might be time to get the investigation under way then." Jeff looked across at me and noticed I was already gathering my equipment ready for the off, as were many of the other team members. Little did we know that Bill's story was only the beginning: the Gaol had plenty more in store for us this night.

Darren and I took the Remand Centre, and although it felt uneasy, all seemed to be quiet for now. Jeff and Bill were busy checking out the yards as they went. It was whilst they were entering Yard 3, that they momentarily paused by the old education centre/kitchen. "Was that a child?" Searching around, only their breath could be seen as they strained to hear if there were any other follow-up noises. For what they had heard upon entering the Yard was a child's voice shouting out what they thought was "Dad".

The Kitchen/Old Education Centre in Yard 3.
(The dark figure is an example of slow shutter speed with a real person)

Ghosts of the Past

"It was all around us," Bill was to explain later. "You couldn't directionalise it."

In the early days of investigating the Gaol, we made a policy of NOT wanting to know anything of her history. This way, if we had something happen we could chat to the Manager, and in return she could maybe verify what we were hearing or seeing with some event from the past. It was a frequent occurrence that we would go to her with something and her answer would be: "That's funny because…" and some information would be passed to us to backup that maybe what had happened could be valid. This child's voice was no exception.

"That's interesting…" the Manager exclaimed, going on to explain that if there was anywhere that we should hear children it would be Yard 3. The reason for this? We were told that in the 1800s it was known for a short while as a family yard. Back then there was no such thing as foster parents, so if you were convicted for stealing that loaf of bread or teaspoon, and you had children, the children would have to come into Gaol with you. This was the yard where apparently the mothers and children were kept away from the other prisoners. But there may also have been another reason for the presence of a child: one that we didn't find out about until many years later. It would not be the first time though, that we would have an indication that there may have been a child involved in the activity during our years there.

Meanwhile back in the New Building, Patrick, who was sitting on the stairs by himself, had heard a rustling coming from the cell next to him. "The whole place felt oppressive," he explained later. The other two investigators who were around the corner in the other part of the building were not feeling any easier. Patrick eventually excused himself from the others and wandered off to join Jeff, who was now in the Bakehouse.

"Why on earth would there be a smell of urine in here?" Jeff said as Patrick entered the Bakehouse. Jeff was busy trying to find the source of the strong smell that was invading his nostrils. He had first smelled it only minutes earlier in the Induction Centre in Yard 3. Megan and he had entered the building and immediately been struck by the stale scent of ammonia. They had thought it strange as although there were toilets and showers in this building, they were disused and the plumbing had been disconnected at the time of the Gaol closure back in 1988. At the time they had dismissed it as maybe lingering smells from years gone by, or maybe the Gaol cats had been the culprits. But in the bakehouse? No toilets here! There was no entry for the cats either as the doors remained locked at all times. There was no conceivable reason for the out-of-place smell, and although a search was made no source was ever found. Just another one of those little mysteries that the Gaol presents from time to time: seemingly small, but always curious. There was nothing to be done but take note and continue the investigation.

The investigation next took Jeff and Patrick to Yard 4. They wandered past the heavy metal door and into the Yard. Whilst poking around they were chatting about the Gaol and how it felt that night. Patrick started to grumble that although it felt uneasy in there, he still was yet to experience anything paranormal on this or on any previous investigations he had been on.

"They could at least slam a door!" he sighed in frustration.

With that said they then turned and entered the Remand Centre, not suspecting for a moment that all hell was about to break loose… The old saying in the Gaol is: "Beware what you ask for!"

—ooo—

"I will be fine here on my own," Megan smiled reassuringly at Darren and me as we were contemplating going back to the Dormitory.

Back in the New Building, our batteries were running their course, and if we were to continue fresh ones were needed. And so it was that Megan now found herself all alone in the New Building: the silence deafening… that is until she heard the shuffling steps that appeared to be coming towards her. Standing near the old metal staircase, she searched the gloom of the block in front of her, hoping to see an explanation. As the shuffling footsteps came closer a new noise was added… a light clunking sound. She strained her ears to try and work out what this could be. The noise suddenly stopped.

"You OK?" a voice said from behind her. Megan had been so focused on what these strange noises could have been that she hadn't heard Darren and myself return to the staircase, and by her expression I could see that something must have just happened before our return.

Explaining what she had just heard, Megan walked down the block, inspecting each door as she went. Her attention rested on the eyepieces that hung on each cell door. The eyepieces had covers over them which, when lifted to one side, would allow a guard to inspect the cell and the prisoner within. It was these eyepiece covers that Megan now realised were the cause of the sound she had just heard. As she lifted one to the side and let it drop, it swung gently before coming to a halt, creating the light clunking sound that had been similar to what she had just been hearing. Had a guard been patrolling and inspecting the prisoners as he always had, this night?

But the footsteps weren't going to stop there. Several times they were heard moving around the New Building this night; at one point so loudly that the three investigators stationed in there were convinced that the other investigators were approaching. They were surprised when nobody appeared. They even called out and did a search, but there was no person to be found.

—ooo—

"Did you hear that?" Patrick and Jeff paused briefly as they entered the museum section of the Remand Centre.

Although the museum sensor light had automatically switched on as they first entered the block, their focus was now firmly on the gloomy and uninviting arched doorway that led to the cellblock beyond. The reason? They thought they had just heard somebody moving around down the far end of the building. Pressing forward, Patrick took the lead, with Jeff not far behind, camcorder poised at the ready.

"HELLO?" Patrick shouted loudly as they stepped over the threshold and into the gloom of the Cellblock itself.

He expected maybe a team member to shout out a reply, but the oppressive and threatening feeling he was now experiencing, told him that there was nobody there… or nobody living that is. He certainly wasn't expecting the reaction to the hello that he was about to receive. As they strained their ears, listening for an answer or even a follow up noise that could explain the cause, the door at the far end began to move. Its momentum grew, and the door slammed shut with a resounding crash which reverberated throughout the building. They hardly had time to wonder on this before the door swung open once more. But this was nothing compared to what greeted them next. As they stood watching, a dark shadowy form of a man glided up the wall towards them before dissolving into nothing, the eerie green glow from the exit signs once more illuminating the figure.

"Did you see that?" Patrick asked in astonishment, hoping that Jeff could confirm that it hadn't just been his imagination running wild.

Momentarily thrown off guard, Jeff glanced at Patrick who was busy describing what he had just seen, which was the shadowy form heading towards them. Shaking with excitement and maybe just a touch of fear, they tried to make sense of this new turn of events. The atmosphere in the building had become intense now, almost angry, making the act of moving forward near impossible – though backing off wasn't an option either. After all, this is what they were there for. As Jeff would describe it later in his own words:

"The atmosphere in the Remand Cell block was very heavy and Patrick and I had a sense of dread. This was the first time whilst investigating the Gaol that I had such a feeling. The feeling that came over me was very hard to describe but to say I never want to experience it again. We were both unable to move forward. We both had the gut feeling that it would be unwise." [Jeff Fausch, P.F.I. report]

Composing himself a little, Jeff turned to Patrick and asked, "What was it you said?"

"All I said was Hello," Patrick replied in a quiet voice.

"HELLO!" Jeff tried it for himself, but the door remained motionless.

Patrick quickly jumped in once more: "HELLO!"

BANG!!

The door, on cue to Patrick's voice, slammed shut, startling them both.

"OK… If there is anybody there can you…." Jeff never got to finish his sentence as the door forcefully swung open, slamming back against the wall. The unwelcome feeling hung heavier in the air. Slowly, taking small steps back, they started to retreat into the museum area.

SLAP!!

Swinging the camera round quickly, Jeff was just in time to capture the very large laminated poster that hung next to the whipping rack, lift right up and crash back against the wall: something that was impossible, as I would demonstrate on future tours. (Lifting up this large poster then letting it drop caused a pocket of air to form underneath, cushioning it from being able to hit the wall with any strength.)

Ghosts of the Past

Large Poster to the left of the whipping rack

BANG! BANG!

Settling back down, the poster was quickly followed by a succession of large bangs as the door at the end slammed shut once more, quickly followed by the heavier door to the side of them. And still the atmosphere became heavier!

"Time to go!" Jeff and Patrick started to back out of the Remand Centre to rejoin the team.

It would be easy at this stage to sit in the comfort of your own home and wonder why – when things were happening all around – that these two team members would chose to leave. In reality, there is probably not one of us who can say how we would truly react if given the same situation. It has to be remembered that it wasn't just what was happening, it was the atmosphere in the Gaol that night – especially in this section. It had a menacing and unwelcome feel, and it is human nature to subconsciously avoid situations that could be a danger. It is our fight/flight response: a response that in our tribal years would have kept us alive.

A Night to Remember

In the heat of a moment your adrenaline starts to pump and your natural instincts take over: in this instance the flight response was strongest for these two men.

This flight response only lasted a short time however, before they gathered themselves together and quickly headed back down to the Remand Section, this time with Bill and Megan accompanying them. Entering through the bottom door, they double-checked to see how freely this door would swing. They soon discovered upon slamming it as hard as had been witnessed, that the door would stick, and a lot of force would be needed to re-open it again. On top of this, although it was possible for the door to move under breezy conditions, on subsequent observations it never moved past the 45 degree angle and certainly couldn't slam back against the wall with such force. This just added to the mystery of how the door reopened so freely on the video. It should be noted that many times on tours I would demonstrate how sticky this door was and allowed people to try and reopen it. However, not long after this, one of the volunteers became sick of the sticky door and planed it so it closes and opens more easily now.

As they stood discussing the problems with the door, Patrick and Bill found themselves breaking out into laugher as they watched Jeff pitch forward with a grunt. Jeff failed to share their amusement however. He had turned his back to the door as they had been in deep discussion, and as he was chatting to the others the door had suddenly flown open, striking him hard in the back and sending him staggering forward and desperately trying to keep his balance. The door then remained still and unmoved. Jeff was later to say that in his opinion "it seemed like a deliberate well-timed act".

"Over there," Bill pointed excitedly towards the museum section. He had just witnessed the shadow of a man once more crossing the dividing door from the cellblock to the museum. Quickly they hurried up the long corridor towards where it had been witnessed. There was nothing to be seen now: however it was noticed that one of the leather wrist straps on the whipping rack was swinging freely, as if recently a hand had been freshly removed from it.

The whole event was captured on videotape. Sadly for us though, the shadow person that came up the wall towards them, didn't register on the actual camera – a frustration that we were to face many times over.

Although this cellblock seemed to be the catalyst for activity that night, and it continued to produce small but interesting phenomena, none were as dramatic as this event. It was as if it had made its point, thrown its tantrum and finally, like a moody child, quietly started to sulk.

—ooo—

"OK guys, I need to call it a night," stretching with an accompanying yawn I started to turn off my camera.

It had already been a reasonably long night and very eventful. However, things appeared to have calmed down and the atmosphere had now eased. I had a husband who needed to go to work early in the morning and children to be seen to, so it was time to depart. Darren agreed that he also needed to go, and so we left the other investigators to it.

Returning to the Remand Centre, Megan, Jeff and Bill started to monitor the area. Whatever had caused the outburst earlier seemed now to be fairly quiet; but that didn't stop Megan from hearing what appeared to be piano playing, a sound that was not finished with them that night.

"Is this a hotspot?" Bill scratched his head.

Having walked further into the Remand and stopping dead centre of the cellblock, the thermometer was now reading several degrees warmer than either side of it. It was puzzling as we had expected cold spots, not areas that suddenly read warmer. Was it a fault with the thermometer? It was a mystery that may have had an explanation – but for this possible explanation we were going to have to wait a little while yet.

It was now 6.00 am and a distant glow in the sky was starting to appear as the night came to a close. Walking back to the Dormitories, the three investigators stopped by Yard 1 which lay at the foot of the stairs leading back up to the Dormitories.

"There it is again, guys," whispered Megan.

Sure enough she could hear the piano playing once more, only this time Jeff was hearing it too.

"Nah, that's just a dripping pipe," Bill looked around to find the source, and pointed to a pipe that indeed had a constant drip.

"No…" Megan shook her head slowly, still listening intently to the sounds she was hearing. "I can hear that too… but this is over the top of the pipe, like old-time piano/organ playing."

It appeared to be coming from all around them in the yard. This is something that was always noticed with sounds in the Gaol over the years: they seem to be non-directional, yet all around you. They continued to listen for close to ten minutes as the melodic sounds filled the air around them. It was later described as old-time classical, or maybe a hymn. To Bill though, it remained a dripping pipe as he heard nothing of the music, despite the other investigators hearing it clearly.

—000—

"Ahhh… the music." The Manager found it interesting to hear of this when we phoned her the next day. Apparently it had been heard before and even on a tour. It is interesting to note that on that occasion, only half the tour could hear the notes being played; the other half heard nothing. One half of the tour was excitedly trying to point out the music whilst the other half scratched their heads and came to the conclusion that these people must be totally mad. We can only conclude that maybe some people are more sensitive to this phenomena than others… or maybe they have a more active imagination? Who knows with the mystery we refer to as the paranormal.

As for the Remand Centre? The Manager had no answers for why this particular section had been so active and almost angry that night. This was just a debtor's prison and an area where people who were awaiting trial were kept; no hardcore prisoners were ever kept there. It was a couple of years later that I may have eventually found a possible answer to this mystery.

The Manager was also at a loss to explain why this date, the 28th June, should have any significance. There were no anniversaries on this date: nothing to explain why such activity should appear to increase there, and especially to turn so hostile. It should be noted that although P.F.I. went back many times on this date, and tours are often booked in on this date each year, we have never experienced the Gaol quite like this since. It was more than enough, however, to convince us that to leave the Gaol now and move on would be inconceivable.

If the Gaol didn't have our full attention before, it certainly did now!

Ghosts of the Past

Overview of the Gaol showing the Visitors' Centre, Watch Tower and Yard 4 Cell Block

Chapter 5
A Finished Hiatus

"I had a feeling of chest pain, tightness, headache, stomach ache and tiredness just before Alison spoke. All these feelings left as I left the main area. I wasn't scared, just the physical sensations felt uncomfortable"

(Jennifer, Ghost Tour)

AHHH... it feels good to be back, I sighed as we stepped into the Gaol once more. For a variety of reasons, it was a further fifteen months before P.F.I. could return to the Gaol to commence another series of investigations. It wasn't until we stood there looking around that we realised just how much we had missed the Old Girl.

Patrick was particularly excited as this would be the maiden voyage of the new trigger device he had just built. He was eager to find out if it was all working smoothly, and what better place to trial it than here in the Gaol, a place where we could monitor the comings and goings of people and influences. As any investigator would know, leaving a camera rolling for many hours means many hours of footage to be trawled through afterwards... scintillating stuff when sometimes all you are looking at is an empty hallway. So Patrick built a device that could be left, often for a week or more, that would monitor an area for us. The great part about it was that it would not be constantly taping, but have sensors that would trigger the VHS video to record for four minutes each time there was a change around the sensors. The principle triggers were looking for changes in Electro Magnetic Fields, audio, infra-red and temperature. It was only later that Theremin was added. VHS was ideal rather than a laptop DVR, as a VHS recorder was more practical to leave running in an unmonitored environment for long periods of time. The drawback to this method though, was it took seconds for the recorder to commence taping, so possibly missing altogether the event that triggered it off.

The device proved over time to be very effective, but not so much for the paranormal. Upon our first trial we found we had noises and shuffling. Future endeavours produced a mobile phone and even a radio playing. These would have to be very 'high tech' ghosts, and I was highly impressed that the spirit world too would need mobile phones!! If it was paranormal it was certainly good to see that they keep up with technology so well! In fact it turned out that we had evidence, not of a ghost, but another entity that had made the Gaol his home: a very much alive resident who in fact was an intruder. We spent nearly 150 years trying to keep people IN the Gaol: the rest of the time we were having problems trying to keep them OUT. After all, there were warm cells and beds still to be found in the buildings, not to mention that the kitchen was full of food and drink, having been hired out to a function centre. As you can imagine, this was much warmer and cosier than sleeping rough in the Parklands. It was never found out who this mysterious person was, but a couple of times we thought we had him, only to find… it wasn't him!

—o0o—

"Would you be willing to take some of our Ghost Tours?" the Manager approached Jeff and me one day. Although there were already volunteers who were conducting the tours, it was felt that more were now very much needed. Over time, with the media interest in the work P.F.I. were conducting and with the P.F.I. website, word was filtering out and people were starting to become more aware of what the Gaol possibly had on offer. We naturally jumped at the idea: after all it meant more time in the Gaol for us, as well as having a captive audience to share our passion with.

And so it was that Jeff and I turned up for our very first tour. It was to be a small tour that night, just a married couple from NSW hoping to have a ghostly experience. With it being our first tour we were fairly excited ourselves, though nerves were also playing a part.

"Hey guys," I said as I strolled into the Remand Centre on my own, ready to set up some equipment so we could show the slamming-door video to the tour. My philosophy when in the Gaol has always been that whether I believed there is anything there or not, it doesn't hurt to hedge your bets and be polite. After all this is their home not mine. "If there is anybody here tonight…" I continued, "please, please can you do something for the tour tonight?" At this stage I truly thought it would be great if they could perform and put in an appearance; not only to give these people an experience, but maybe to help our credibility. How cool would it be for something to happen: maybe footsteps, a fleeting glimpse of a figure, banging doors… not much to ask, I thought. I wasn't choosey, but it appeared that they were!

Our guests for the night arrived, a lovely couple who were impressed and delighted with the Gaol as they wandered around listening to our ghostly tales, and fascinated by the investigation stories we included – all the time being harassed by Doc, one of the Gaol cats. Doc was a lovely cat who was very much a people cat. He would often accompany us on our tours, preferring our company rather than wandering off on his own, unlike the other cat, Clink. Both nearly identical in their striking ginger coats, Doc could always be picked out easily, as he was never far from the person who he would adopt for the night. But this night he was behaving oddly. He would come up to us, obviously agitated; something we had never witnessed Doc do before. He was meowing, but instead of the friendly meow and rub he would normally give, he was making his utterances in a more urgent way and he would immediately turn and wander back to the shop area. As he became more desperate and more demanding we tried to shoo him away as it was very distracting to the flow of storytelling.

Finally, two hours later, the tour came to a close, and we arrived back at the shop, with the guests eager to write in the visitor's book and buy their souvenirs. This was also where I proceeded to learn my lesson.

"Erm… It's locked," I said, trying desperately to open the shop door, "but we didn't lock this!"

As Jeff stepped forward and also tried the handle, it soon dawned on us that the door had locked itself from the inside – something we would never have been so foolish to do surely?

Glancing back at the now nervous guests, I smiled reassuringly, "It's OK though, we have the master keys to open it". I paused as I noticed Jeff pull back from looking through the shop window whilst slowly shaking his head at me. "Or maybe not…" I added weakly.

The keys were now sitting boldly on the counter inside the shop. The very keys that locked the Gaol, and set the security, were teasing us well out of reach. I exchanged a worried glance with Jeff. How were we going to explain this one to the Manager, that on our first tour we seemingly had stuffed up.

"You're putting this on…" a worried voice came from behind us, quickly reminding us that we still had the tour people and that we now couldn't unlock any doors to let them out. As I turned round to reassure them I noticed they were pointing and looking up at the ceiling above us. It was then that we too heard what they were eluding to… footsteps! Heavy, slow and methodical, walking across the floor above us. Doc left quickly, leaving the four of us standing there with our mouths gaping, staring at the ceiling above us.

"Tell us you are putting this on…" the guest interrupted again. At this point she obviously didn't know whether she should be scared or excited.

"Erm… it's not us doing this," I promised, as I watched Jeff move off, mobile phone in hand.

A few minutes later he returned with news from the Manager. An alternative way into the shop had been explained; along with the fact she had greeted this news with amusement – not anger. Fortunately for us, she had experienced the same thing happen to her a short time before; only this time she had been IN the shop dealing with the money when the door had closed and locked itself from the outside. The damage to the doorframe where she had to break out with a screwdriver is still there to this day.

Could one of the rumoured 'ghosts' be using us for his amusement that night? There is a twist to the story: we were told that in the records it apparently states that Governor Ashton was a bit of a trickster with a strong sense of humour. He was well-known for playing practical jokes on both the prisoners and the staff who worked there. Could it be that he still continues to this day? I did learn my lesson though: NEVER ask them to perform like circus animals!

The moral of the story? Beware what you ask for in the Gaol.

—oOo—

It was also on one of our tours not long after this that we thought we had finally caught the intruder!

A thunderstorm had passed through Adelaide hours before a tour was due to commence. Jeff had arrived at the Gaol earlier than myself, and he had gone to the Remand Centre to set up the video and TV once again to show the tour the footage. It was whilst plugging it in that Jeff froze momentarily.

"I know you!" a male voice whispered loudly.

Reaching for his camera, he was convinced the intruder must be in the building with him. Swinging round quickly, he took a photograph in the vain hope that he at least would be able to get a picture of the intruder before he was possibly attacked. Nothing! Nobody was there and there was no place for them to hide. Looking back on the photograph though, a misty grey form seems to have been caught up in the rafters.

Having arrived shortly after this incident, Jeff and I were standing at the Gaol waiting for a tour which didn't show, mainly due to the flooding problems on the road caused by the heavy rain. Rather than go home, we decided that an impromptu investigation would be in order and we quickly called some of the team members to come down. When else were we going to get the chance to be there on the premises after a well-timed thunderstorm? It was an opportunity to see if Hollywood is correct and see if there is an increase in the phenomena during thunderstorm activity.

Having negotiated our way around the flooded Sallyport, we now stood in the laneway not far from the old metal staircase leading up to the Chapel where we discussed the plan of action for the night.

"Who's that man...!" It was more an exclamation of surprise than a question.

We paused in the discussion we were having to look at Megan, who had just interrupted and was now standing staring towards the tunnel door, a puzzled look on her face. She went on to explain that she had just witnessed a man shuffling through the laneway, head bowed and hands in pockets. She had watched as he had turned direction and entered the long tunnel that led to the New Building. Megan was later to tell us:

"I saw a person walking along next to the wall leading up to the tunnel in the New Building. He was heading towards me before entering through the doorway of the tunnel. He was wearing dark clothing; either black or dark-blue slacks plus a jacket and what looked like a beanie hat. He was walking slowly with hands in his pockets, head bowed, and taking shuffling steps"

"Be careful, it may be the intruder!" I shouted after Megan who was now heading rapidly towards the tunnel. I glanced at Jeff and then we quickly followed. If it was the intruder we knew he was trapped! The tunnel is long and has no doors leading off it. At the far end is another large, heavy gate that we KNEW was still locked. We had him, he was cornered at last!!

Somewhat hesitantly we drew close to the entrance; I say hesitantly because there was the nagging thought that this person could turn out to be violent or dangerous.

Ghosts of the Past

The mysterious shoe print left in the tunnel

Due to Megan describing him as 'solid', the concept of 'ghost' had never entered our heads. This was soon to change however, as we stood at the entrance looking at a now completely empty tunnel. Empty, that is, except for one lone shoe print, carefully placed half way up the tunnel. Despite it being a wet night, there were no shoe prints leading up to it and none after: just a single step, so fresh that it even had drip marks after the toe. Was it Jeff's, he had been the only male there that night? Well we did compare the prints between Jeff's shoe and the mysterious shoe print, only to find that they were not only a different size but that one had a heel and the other was a flat shoe. So who was this man? Well we can only assume at this point, as the Manager did verify that the clothing described would have been worn by the prisoners at the later stage of the Gaol's working life.

But the shoe prints didn't stop at this single incident on the night. Later in the evening the three of us wandered over to the Remand Centre and found that shoe prints seemed to be the theme for the night. We have noted that if we have something happen in a night, often it will re-occur again in the same evening… but then may never happen again. This particular night looked like it was going to be no different.

A Finished Hiatus

"Are these what I think they are?" I peered closer at what looked to be small bare foot prints on the cement of the floor of the museum area.

Tala, my German Shepherd, was with me on this occasion and I had allowed her to wander around to see if she could pick anything up. I quickly called her away from the area where the prints were; but not before she left comparison size prints next to these foot prints. This proved to be a vital comparison, as we watched the moisture from the dog's foot prints blur and blend into the cement – much like you would expect from water on cement. But still, the small bare foot prints stayed crisp as if stained into the cement.

Placing my foot next to these foot prints for comparison, we could deduce that they were either a very small female or a child, as they were at least a couple of sizes smaller than my own. Even more baffling, was the fact that of the four prints displayed on the floor, the first three all seemed to be of a left foot in a line; then off to one side was a print of the right foot – almost as if a child had been playing the game of hopscotch moments before we had entered. We busied ourselves taking photographs and decided to check on them later. The foot prints remained

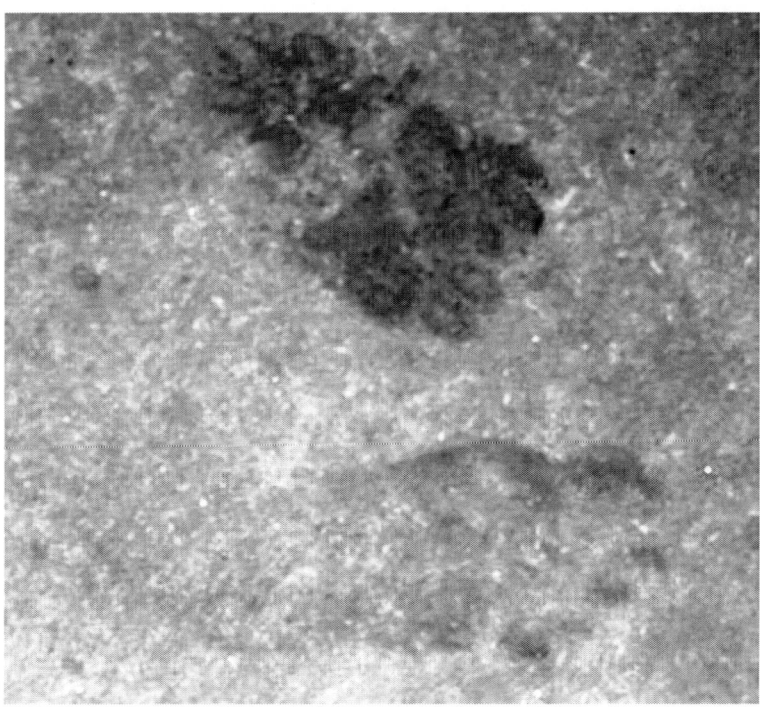

Tala's foot print at top and the small bare foot print below

for the rest of the night; and in fact they remained for several days after this before suddenly disappearing as mysteriously as they had appeared. We were to come across these small bare foot prints once more during our time at the Gaol.

"Oh those... Strange you should say that." Many years later, the caretaker we were chatting to one night eagerly picked up his torch and beckoned us to follow: "I can show you them again," he stated.

We had been chatting to him about our findings over the investigations, and the topic of the strange foot prints had come up. We now followed him into the New Building and waited patiently as he unlocked the secured gate leading up the old metal staircase. We soon found ourselves standing next to the hanging beam and trapdoor.

"There you go," the caretaker's torchlight danced off the floor and sure enough, sitting quietly in the years of dust and dirt, were small bare foot prints, as if a child had curiously wandered in and out between the mannequins.

So if these WERE the foot prints of a child, it raised the question: what on earth would a child have been doing in these areas? Children were indeed kept in the Gaol without a doubt. Sometimes because they had committed some misdeed themselves, but often they accompanied those mothers who had committed a crime but had no family members to take on their children.

Checking in with the Manager the next day, we were told that the museum area had once been a part of Yard 5, an area where children were incarcerated in when they had committed crimes such as pick pocketing etc. Could one child still be remaining?

Overall though, this was the most active night we had come up against since the famous June 28th that kept us at the Gaol originally. We appeared to get audible voices, full apparitions and physical evidence of something unusual going on.

Maybe Hollywood is right after all about one thing: severe thunder and lightning, and the atmospheric conditions that follow, DO appear to increase possible paranormal activity!

—oOo—

This also seems like a good time to bring up another theory: remembering that a 'theory' is all that the subject of the paranormal can ever be at this stage.

A Finished Hiatus

There is an old kitchen area in the Gaol that I have always disliked ever since I had the bad experience there on my first tour. A couple of years ago the floor in that kitchen suddenly collapsed, and the Gaol found that it was more historically important than once was believed. Archaeologists from the Adelaide University came in and found evidence that there had been settlements prior to the Gaol in this area, both European and Aboriginal. The first settlers to arrive in the Colony set out streets which were lined with temporary dwellings, and instead of clearing these settlements on commencement of building the Gaol, they just capped them. Under the floors of the Gaol there is still evidence of communities long gone, and some of the items which have been discovered are now displayed at the Gaol. Wedding rings, human teeth, pottery and even carved sheep bones have been found amongst other things in only a small section of the kitchen area. One can only wonder what else lies under the nine acres of floor and yards of the Adelaide Gaol. But back to the theory. Could it be that what is often seen in the Gaol, and does not fit into Gaol history and routine, is from a time period BEFORE the Gaol was even built? Were these 'ghosts' from the past already here as the floors were being laid and the walls being built? Could this be the reason for a child and a lady in grey being heard and seen in areas where children and ladies were never allowed?

—o0o—

"I am going to have to go home to fix this one," Patrick said as he stood scratching his head. He had just found out that the programme that ran his sensor equipment, and in particular the security cameras, has just erased itself. What was most baffling was the fact that he had just checked and tested it that very day. "It can't be fixed here, but I will be back soon," and with that Patrick left the Gaol temporarily. We were now into February 2005.

As Bill and I had teamed up, Jeff now found himself wandering alone towards the Hanging Tower. It was whilst he was taking photos opposite the Hanging Tower that one of the metal signs started to shake violently in front of him. Startled, he moved towards it, noting that it was a still night and there wasn't a breath of wind to be felt. As it stopped moving he curiously tried to recreate the sound, only to find a fair bit of force was needed to acquire the same effect.

Meanwhile Bill and I were monitoring the alleyway in the hope of a repeat visit from Megan's figure, or 'Beanie Man' as he had now come to be known. Sitting quietly we observed the length of the alleyway. At first it seemed quiet, but slowly it dawned on us that we could hear murmured voices coming from the side of us.

Ghosts of the Past

The surgery

Straining our ears harder we followed the sounds to the Medical Centre. Men talking in low voices like murmurs in another room: definitely voices, but we were unable to make out what they were saying. Walking round to the surgery door we turned the handle to enter, only to find that the door was locked. There was certainly nobody inside to be having a conversation. With our rattling of the door, the surgery fell silent once more.

"I think Jeff is down there," I pointed down towards the end of the alleyway where I had just heard footsteps coming from. "He must be round the corner, we should go join him and tell him about the voices." We wandered down, half expecting to collide with Jeff as he came around the corner, but nothing. Jeff was nowhere to be seen and was apparently still in the Hanging Tower at this time. Shaking our heads at the subtle sounds we seemed to be hearing that night, we returned to the Sallyport and stood discussing where to next…

THUD!!!

A loud noise on the floor above us caused us to jump. It sounded as if something heavy had been thrown to the ground with some force. Sadly we were unable to go upstairs and into the Governor's old quarters due to the fact it had been rented out to an artist at the time…an artist who was only present in the Gaol during daylight hours.

"What's up?" both Bill and myself jumped as Jeff came up behind us.

We discussed the sounds and the footsteps, and for awhile we listened in the dark, but the only sounds were our breathing… nothing more eventuated. It was time to move on we decided.

The bell ringing told us that Patrick had finally returned. He was still very confused as to why the trigger programme had wiped itself clean. He explained that there should even have been a battery backup in case of power failure. The important thing was that it was now working, and the best place to set it up was obviously going to be the New Building, so that is where we headed next.

In the course of an investigation we can take hundreds of photographs. As we all stagger out at the end of the night with retina burn, we know how annoying the flashes can be to us. However, if there is another realm with 'ghosts and spirits' we really don't know how it would affect them, if at all – but it is possible we may have found out on this particular night in the New Building!

After setting up the trigger devices again, Patrick and I settled down on the staircase, whilst Jeff focused on the Guards' Quarters at the top of the stairs, carefully positioning himself between the tripods that were holding our cameras and sensors. At this stage I was sitting on the third step down, and as I sat snuggled into my coat, the warmth it brought caused a drowsiness to sweep over me. Embarrassingly, I have been caught on film several times taking a micro-sleep. Fellow investigators will know well that wall of exhaustion that hits at some point of a long night. Your body tells you darkness has fallen, sleep is now essential and it is a struggle to stop the head from falling and the eyes from closing. Once that wall is hurdled however, the 'second wind' normally appears and off you go again. So it was I found myself in that half-world of sleep… a world where you are still conscious of all that is going on around you even though you are totally relaxed. I was still fully aware of the clicking of Jeff's camera behind me and how it seemed to be never ending. And then I heard it…

"Enough's enough!"

A deep authoritative male voice echoed through my head. And for fear of the readers thinking I had gone mad… I will admit that it wasn't an external voice: it was very much IN my head – something, I might add, that has never happened to me before or since. I stress that I am certainly not prone to 'hearing voices'. A split second later I was pulled back to full consciousness as Jeff exploded backwards nearly knocking our equipment off the tripods and stumbling over the video and trigger equipment behind him. Recovering himself from an obvious shock, he explained to us that he had pushed his camera hand through the bars and had been taking photo after photo when a cold, clammy hand had wrapped itself around his and pushed his hand down. He described how he could even clearly feel the fingers and thumb wrapping themselves round his wrist as it happened. Coincidentally, it was the exact moment I had heard the male voice in my head say "Enough's enough". Is it possible that camera flashes annoy them just as much us? I guess until the day we can personally talk to them, we will never know.

—o0o—

Winter started to creep in and before we knew it, we were into July 2004. As had become the norm, P.F.I. were in yet again on a Sunday as this was proving to be the quietest night away from the hustle and bustle of the frequent tours and sleepovers. As usual, the team members did a sweep of the Gaol first, closing doors and turning off lights as they went so that we knew if we had any open doors or lights turned on, then it wasn't us. As they wandered around it was also at the back of their minds that the intruder could still be very much present; and why when Jeff walked into Yard 3 the black shadowy form he witnessed was assumed to be just this person. As Jeff watched the shadowy figure move behind the still-open door of the Education Centre, he knew yet again that the intruder was trapped. There was definitely nowhere to hide this time! But once again the person had disappeared, this time seemingly through solid walls. Jeff found himself searching an empty yard with empty buildings.

Moments later Megan entered the yard and noticed Jeff busily searching for something and looking confused, yet relieved, that there had been no sign of what could have been a violent intruder. As she walked towards him a movement caught her eye from the second floor of the cell block. She was later to describe it as a "whitish form" that did not have a shape, yet it appeared to freely move along the upper balcony. The night ahead seemed like it was already starting to show great promise.

However, time passed and although they were getting temperature and EMF [Electro Magnetic Field] fluctuations, nothing tangible was being experienced. It was noted, though, that the two-way radios had started to malfunction whilst in Yard 3. Over the years this was to be a common problem, especially in the

A Finished Hiatus

Toilet block

Induction Centre, and tonight seemed to prove no different. At the end of the night though, although it started off with promise, very little eventuated.

The following investigation, again on the Sunday, proved more fruitful. Leaving half the team to set up in the New Building, Megan and Jeff returned once again to Yard 3 to take readings and get a feel for the atmosphere there that night. As they were doing the readings there was a sudden bang from the adjacent Yard 2. Megan immediately went to check it out but could find no obvious cause for such a loud noise. Jeff, following through minutes later, paused… what was that noise that he was now hearing clearly close to the more modern toilet block?

"Did you say something?" Megan turned to Jeff, expecting him to repeat what she thought she had just heard him say. But there it was again, and this time Jeff hadn't moved or spoken, as she was looking directly at him.

"Did you hear that?" Jeff asked Megan, whilst looking around for the source of the noise he was presently hearing.

Ghosts of the Past

On our investigations we refrain from disclosing exactly what we are hearing until after. This way we don't put ideas into another investigator's head. Later, notes are exchanged and similarities explored. In this case, it appeared that although both investigators were hearing some sort of sounds, both were hearing it in a different way. Megan told of how she was hearing voices, and at first thought it had been Jeff due to him being the only other person in her vicinity. However, it soon dawned on her that what she was hearing was more like chanting. It was reminiscent of those schoolyard days when fights would break out, students would gather, and they would edge the combatants on: "Fight, fight, fight!" We probably all remember those, and I would guess that things have not changed over the years. Jeff, however, was hearing a different sound: what he was hearing was a rhythmic banging noise, much like pots being clanged, and as the kitchen loomed over them in this yard, it would probably be an area this would have been heard. Had there been a fight situation in this spot, where the prisoners methodically edged it on by banging pots and chanting? There were probably many over time. Maybe what they were hearing was residual sounds from years gone by.

"That's strange, my camera won't focus!" Jeff quizzically played with his settings on the video camera, but each time he pointed it at the toilet block the picture blurred and he had to turn it away to focus the picture once more. Giving up, he picked up the still camera – only to find that this too was unable to focus in the general area of the toilet block. Giving up on the toilet block he diverted his attention to the old kitchen.

"Can you bring up that last picture?" Megan asked, an element of surprise in her voice.

Jeff scrolled back to the previous picture and passed the camera over to her. "I just saw this with the naked eye," she exclaimed.

Being a seasoned investigator Jeff had kept the camera at arms length and held his breath while taking the photograph. Dust? It is probably the most sensible answer: but it does leave a mystery as to why Megan saw it illuminated in the flash with the naked eye. She later went on to describe it as a "large misty sphere that was larger than a softball".

"Oh you have to be kidding me!" Megan had been taking photos around the toilet block on her own a short time later, when a new sound was heard. In Megan's words it sounded like "somebody having a wee".

Thinking it was one of the male investigators, she stormed over to the toilet block to give them a piece of her mind… more so because she knew we couldn't clean the urinal as the water had been disconnected to this toilet block back when the Gaol shut down in 1988. Reaching the doorway she drew in a breath ready to say something, only to slowly exhale it as she stood looking at the empty room. As she stood there, the sound continued for a few seconds more: obviously whoever it was, was desperate after all these years! She turned around and searched the yard and noticed the small group of male investigators standing around chatting at the far end in the gloom. Megan called out to Jeff, and once more they found themselves standing by the toilet block.

So, why did we get so much activity this night round the toilet block? Well, we returned on that date the following year, and in fact many times over the years, but we never caught or heard those sounds again. Maybe it was just random residual noises, maybe from an event that had turned violent in that area: after all, we have all watched the movies and the TV shows… If something is going to happen to a prisoner it is often in a toilet block or shower that it takes place.

Ghosts of the Past

The Laneway leading from the Sallyport

Chapter 6
The Ghost Tours Continue

"Standing outside the toilet area, my Dad and myself heard a piece of glass shake which made us look up, only to see the metal gate had started shaking also."

(Samuel, Ghost Tour)

I REALLY do look forward to our tours now, I reflected happily whilst trying to pin my Adelaide Gaol identity badge to my coat. I winced as I missed the coupling and hit my finger instead. A couple of months had passed, and we were definitely getting into the swing of taking the tours. There was something uplifting about being able to share your passion with up to twenty other people who were all prepared to listen. We are all storytellers at heart, and belong to a unique species of creatures that love to do this. The human race is a species of storytellers which dates back to our bonding rituals around the tribal campfires. In fact we still do it today, only the campfires have been replaced by Facebook, MySpace and other network and blogging sites. This category of storytelling also includes books, such as the one you are reading now.

That night we had an all-ladies night coming and, although we were looking forward to it, we already suspected it may be a difficult one. In our early days there, a local hotel/restaurant hired the Gaol for functions and had their own marquee set up. Tonight was one of those nights that the tour would clash with a function. We crossed our fingers and hoped that the two wouldn't interfere with each other too much.

It wasn't long before the 24 lovely ladies turned up, full of fun and excitement and having obviously already communed with 'spirits' of a different kind! This was no more apparent than when they all lined themselves up in the tunnel leaving a small, and only just accessible, path for Jeff to walk through to unlock the gate that still remained shut at the far end. As Jeff made his way through the sea of ladies – who just couldn't resist keeping their hands to themselves – his speed increased and he was obviously very much relieved to have finally made his way through. The gate swung open and the tour headed through to the New Building.

Standing on the stairs, I proceeded to tell the stories of the guard and his ghostly footsteps… "Shush," one of the ladies said urgently. In mid-sentence I stopped, and we all strained our ears to try and catch what the lady was thinking she was hearing. There they were: the unmistakable sound of heavy boots.

"It is probably just somebody from the function," I suggested casually. Patrick, who had joined us for the night, hurried off to check but came back shaking his head and shrugged. Just in case though, he positioned himself so he had full view to all three wings of the T-shaped building. It wasn't long before the footsteps returned; echoing through the building seemingly from a person unseen. This was my first introduction to the footsteps that I had often heard about and it wouldn't be the last, although the next three times would be a lot more dramatic.

Satisfied that they may have been witness to something paranormal, we moved away from the function area and continued our way around the Gaol.

Walking into the Recreation Room, which separates Yards 2 and 3, I handed over the storytelling to Jeff for a time and sneaked off on my own into Yard 3. Often I would leave the tour to wander ahead and take photographs, or just stand to soak in the atmosphere of the Old Girl herself. Positioning myself off to one side of the old Education Centre, I started to snap off some shots. My finger hesitated suddenly, part way to pressing the shutter button down. What was that I had just seen… movement up on the top level of the cellblock? Lowering the camera I quickly turned towards the image that had just attracted my attention. What appeared to be a misty grey form at the top of the staircase, rapidly disappeared as my line of sight became full on with it. Now it was gone. Witnesses of these phenomena often describe as seeing it in their peripheral vision. It is much like looking at a star, it appears clearer when we look off-centre to this object. The theory behind this is that our eye is made up of different cells at different points of the eye. Some are cone shaped and others are rod shaped. It is thought that one type of these cells will pick up the image whereas the other won't. The impression I got in this case was that it was female – but I can't explain why I would suggest this, as I did not get a clear view of it. I did, however, make the decision NOT to discuss what I had just seen with the tour. If I had said, "Hey guys, guess what: I just saw a ghost and you missed it," it would sound incredibly tacky and people obviously would think I had made it up specifically for the tour. So I decided silence was the order of the night and I would just discuss it privately with Jeff

The Ghost Tours Continue

at the end of the tour. Hearing the tour approaching, I ceased the photos and stepped to one side to allow them through.

"Oh, did anybody else see that?" an astonished lady pointed up to the far corner of the upper balcony.

"See what?" I asked innocently, already suspecting what it was she may have seen.

"I just saw the figure of a lady at the top of the balcony up there," she replied, still pointing to the exact same spot I had witnessed my 'form'.

Hitting the air silently, I smiled and then proceeded to tell my story to the tour – both of us relieved that we had not been alone in our vision. Since this time, her mother has returned on a tour, and I quickly handed over the storytelling to her for a change.

The Turning Circle with yard doors.

Ghosts of the Past

Merrily the ladies had made their way around the Gaol: but one smaller incident was to occur before the night was through. It should be noted that each yard finishes back at the Turning Circle, much like wedges of a cake, and it was to the Turning Circle we had then moved to. Once more I took up the role of storyteller whilst Jeff stood back keeping a discreet distance and a very close eye on the audience.

"People often feel like…" I stopped mid-sentence as a lady stooped down and picked up a red plastic light cover from one of the buttons on the door.

"Who threw this at us?" she turned to Jeff accusingly, who could only shrug and look at it in puzzlement. The small red light cover screws into its usual position: yet on this occasion, it had managed to make a sudden journey of approximately six metres across the yard to land perfectly in the middle of this group of ladies.

We all just stood staring at it in silence. None of us had thrown it; and even if it had unthreaded, it would have simply dropped to the floor, not flown across such a large distance. It was the first time that night that I heard the ladies go quiet… and blissfully it remained that way for the rest of the tour.

—ooo—

"Well, it looks like they aren't coming". I glanced at the clock on the wall that now was reading 30 minutes past the tour start time. Yet again a thunderstorm had hit Adelaide, and the accompanying torrential rain had flooded roads enough to dissuade people from travelling. Of course we had to be there whatever, just in case, and now there we were with no tour. We decided that we should relock the Gaol and call it a night; but as always we went armed with cameras in the hope of attaining that elusive shot.

It was as we entered the Turning Circle that we paused: there was a strong smell of burning. I live in a house with an open fire, and I would definitely have described it as burning wood. Strange, as there are no homes around the Gaol, only parkland. What was stranger still, was that the smell was only present in the Turning Circle. As we moved out of this area, so did the smell. It remained only a short time and it disappeared as quickly as it had come. This was going to be my first introduction to this smell: a further experience was yet to be had.

It was as we entered Yard 4 that we were taken by surprise that night. As soon as we entered the yard it felt different; a feeling of anxiety started to spread over

The Ghost Tours Continue

me. Not saying anything to Jeff, we stepped into the yard and split up – after all if something felt uncomfortable then this was where we needed to be. For the first time it felt like hard work trying to go further into the yard, and the feeling intensified the further I walked in. Suddenly I was gripped by an inability to breathe: I physically could not expand my diaphragm to take in air and my lungs started to hurt. Panic started to build, which did not help the situation in anyway, and I was rooted to the spot struggling for air. Just as I was about to call to Jeff, there was a flash of light and the feeling lifted and was gone. The air felt light once more around me, and my chest expanded feeling the pleasure of oxygen passing through once more.

"I just had the weirdest experience," Jeff said as I rapidly joined him. He explained exactly what I had been feeling, and had actually panicked himself as he had assumed he was suffering from some medical condition. He told how he had taken a photo with his camera and the feeling had suddenly left – not only him, but seemingly the yard itself. This at least explained the flash of light. The rest of the evening we spent walking around freely with no other feelings of dread.

As usual we contacted the Manager the next morning, not only to fill her in on the lack of a tour, but also of the strange experience that we had encountered in Yard 4. She thought about it for a moment before bringing up a part of the history of the Gaol that we had not known. Yard 4 contains the oldest cellblocks and in 1895 there had been a fire in the large building which we now refer to as the Dining Hall. Having caused major damage, the building was then used as a wood storage area; but once again in 1895 the wood caught alight causing another fire. Could this be connected with our feelings? It was a choking inability to breathe that we were feeling just prior to smelling the strong wood odour: were we picking events up from back in time?

—ooo—

Halloween 2004 was upon us, and it seemed natural that the Gaol was approached by the media once more to do a 'Halloween Special'. Once again Channel 7 wanted to interview P.F.I. about their ongoing work at the Gaol as well as follow the Ghost Tour around for the night.

This night we had a tour of 27 students and teachers from New South Wales, and prior to their arrival the camera crew had completed our interviews and were now readying for the tour.

For an hour they trailed around after us and the well-behaved group of children. Although there seemingly wasn't anything startling happening, it was as we went into Yard 4 that things changed. After discussing the story about the light that seemingly comes on on its own in the top corner cell, the tour proceeded up the stairs for a closer look. I hung back to ensure that nobody was left down below as a safety issue, before following them up the cold slate staircase.

"Did anybody just turn that light on?" Apparently as the group approached the cell, the light was on, shining brightly for all to see. We were all more than aware that this light had not been on earlier, before making our way up. It was questionable that maybe one of the kids was playing a prank for the cameras; but was even more questionable when we started to have small stones bounce through the bars and hit the floor in front of us. They appeared to be coming from down below, and I knew there was nobody left down there able to do this. On the video itself you can hear me ask: "Did anybody throw those stones?" to which the tour denied any knowledge. A kids prank once more? Maybe. Several times now people on the tours have been hit by small stones from behind. The last time this happened, some joker at the back of the tour had decided it would be fun to pick up the small stones off the yard and flick them at the tour as it walked out to scare them. The only problem with this was that he was apparently hit from behind by a bigger stone – when no culprit was behind to be seen. A bit of Gaol justice maybe!

It was a week or so later that Jeff stumbled across an article in the *Sunday Mail* newspaper entitled 'Old Haunts'. It talked about how the producer and host of the TV show had 'freaked out' as they were going through the footage they had taken of the Adelaide Gaol. Apparently the footage taken in one section of the Gaol had strong interference whenever they tried to film in there. There had been no problem at all with the rest of the footage taken in other parts of the Gaol; just this one area. They had apparently not been able to film anything useable in there. The section they were filming in? The Induction Centre – the one building where it is almost guaranteed that there will be interference with equipment or battery drainage so common on our tours!

—o0o—

It wasn't long after this that we had to deal with a form of the media yet again. This time two documentary makers wanted to get a feel for the Gaol as they were eager to do something on the 'ghosts' there. So, it was down to Jeff and me to take them for their own private Ghost Tour.

The Ghost Tours Continue

The Induction Centre

It had now rolled on to 2005, and at this time there was a question mark on the future of the Gaol. A dark, black cloud hung over her, and it was a worrying period for us all. The cost of keeping the building open and maintaining it was under question, and it was making us volunteers very nervous. You can only imagine the fondness the volunteers have for this place and for its history. She draws you in and embraces you, and suddenly you find yourself dedicated to her preservation. And this was no different for me.

And so it was that I broke my own rule. The rule that stated I would never ask them to perform like a circus animal again on a tour. The rule that had taught me to be careful what I ask for.

"I am just going to get a torch," I smiled at the two gentlemen who were now standing chatting to Jeff and eager to commence their tour.

I wandered into the office and picking up the torch I temporarily leaned against the desk and looked around.

"OK guys," I took a deep breathe, "I know I said we wouldn't ask again but…"

I proceeded to explain the situation to them and who we had with us that night. I pointed out how important this was to both them and us, as we were fighting to keep their home open and in one piece. I pointed towards the door and the people out of sight, and spoke on how sceptical these two documentary makers were, and how important the project would be to bring the plight of the Gaol to the public's attention. Then with another deep breathe I added, "so guys… if you can do anything to convince them then PLEASE do it tonight!"

With that, I walked back to the shop and rejoined the tour. "Ready?" I smiled.

The tour proceeded, and as Jeff told some stories I glanced around hoping to see some sign that they may have heard me. I strained my ears to listen for any footfalls or voices… nothing! They obviously weren't going to help the situation, so it would be down to us to capture these gentlemen's imaginations instead.

It was in Yard 3 that one of the gentlemen shuddered and began to look uneasy. His colleague asked if he was alright, to which he replied: "I just felt like somebody stroked my cheek". He went on to describe how part of his face had suddenly become very cold, as if a feminine hand had stroked it – certainly with more pressure than a simple breeze.

I hung back a little and gave a small private smile. 'That was great,' I thought to myself, 'now if we could just have something a little more convincing…?' With that we continued the tour.

The final destination on any of our tours is the New Building, the subject of more reported incidents than any other in the Gaol complex. This tour was no exception. Nearing the end we wandered into its gloomy exterior, the only lighting being the green glow cast from the exit signs. Taking up my usual position on the iron staircase, with Jeff sitting to my side, I proceeded to tell the stories to the two men standing directly in front of me.

As I spoke of the guard who is commonly reported at the top of the stairs, a strange expression started to spread across the two faces in front of me. I hesitated in my storytelling and turned my attention to the direction they were now looking. I craned my neck to look into the dark at the top of the stairs. There it was… unmistakable footsteps, distant at first, but seemingly drawing closer. The surrounding silence that had now enveloped us as we listened was so great you could have heard a pin drop. All we could hear were the footsteps; clearer because they had no other noise to compete with.

'Wow,' I thought to myself, feeling a little jolt of excitement, 'this is just splendid timing'. Expecting the footsteps to stop at the top of the stairs, I truly thought this was a good enough spectacle to convince these sceptical documentary makers to proceed with their project; nothing more would be needed. The footsteps stopped at the top of the stairs as expected, and assuming that the show would now be over, I turned back smiling to face our guests once more.

"Well, there's someth…." I stopped mid-sentence. Was I really hearing what I thought I was hearing? The sounds of heavy boots, the click of the heel, the squeak of the leather were now filling the air around us once more… drawing closer… slowly I turned, half expecting to see a dark figure walking down the stairs towards me. Nothing. Yet there it was, the sound of footsteps coming closer, clearly walking down the staircase towards our small group. Speechless, our mouths held open, we listened as it walked right between Jeff and me. Every hair on my right arm physically reacted and rose, as if a static breeze had passed by. The two men at the foot of the stairs stepped aside from each other, and we all listened as the footsteps proceeded down the section and faded as they approached the door at the far end, finally disappearing altogether. The two men later explained they felt the need to step aside and let whatever it was through, as it felt like an authoritative figure.

Needless to say, they were blown away with their experience, as was I. It was so beautifully choreographed and exactly what was needed. As they left the building chatting with excitement, I again hung back and glanced up the stairs. Grinning, I quietly thanked them. This time it appeared that asking had achieved results of the right kind. Maybe it was because this time I asked for the right reasons and didn't just mindlessly ask them to perform like a circus animal for a tour.

These days, I have gone back to my usual rule: I just don't ask!

The whipping rack and leg irons

Chapter 7
Winds of Change

"I thought I could see a poster of a face on the door, but when I looked away and looked back it was gone. When I went upstairs to look it wasn't there and I felt uncomfortable and itchy all over."
(Amy, Ghost Tour)

DURING the hotter months of early 2005 things appeared to be calm with no incidents worthy of discussion. But the investigations continued, and as the colder months drew in, things seemingly picked up once more.

"This is Michael," Jeff introduced our newest member to Patrick and Colin. Michael, like a lot of new members, started off keen, but eventually dropped by the wayside when the reality of what investigation work was really about sunk in. The long hours of nothing but quietly monitoring in silence are not for everybody. Coupled with the hours needed to listen to the audio and watch the video footage after each investigation… well you soon come to realise it isn't quite as glamorous as first thought. Trust me, sitting watching nothing but a hallway for 2-3 hours takes a lot of dedication… and a LOT of caffeine!!

But for now Michael was eager, and the Gaol was always a great place to trial any new member.

The Goal wasn't shy at introducing herself to Michael that night. Having been in the New Building with Colin, Michael had needed to check something with Jeff. Entering the long tunnel, and reaching half way down…

BANG!!!!

Leaping to one side and spinning round he found the large heavy metal gate had slammed shut behind him: strange considering there had only been a light breeze that night. Heart pounding, he took a step back only to pause… were those footsteps approaching? He turned now to look at the open entrance in front of him as the footstep became louder, half expecting to see a dark figure to be suddenly blocking what looked to be his only escape.

"What was that?" Jeff entered the tunnel with Patrick close behind and Michael sighed with relief.

The sheer force of the gate slamming had reverberated into the caretaker's room where Jeff and Patrick had been setting up and testing some new video equipment. They had quickly come to investigate what had slammed so loudly.

"The door just slammed behind me." Michael had quickly regained his composure now that he had others with him.

They moved up to the door and swung it open once more to the position in which it had been sitting. They momentarily waited, half expecting to see some free movement, but nothing. The door remained still. Jeff gave it a quick push and the door appeared to start to shut, but the momentum slowed after a few inches. Returning it to the starting point, Jeff gave it a harder push. Still the door lost momentum and would slow to a halt long before hitting the frame. They scratched their heads a little. The effort Jeff had put in was certainly more forceful then any breath of wind that had been present that night! In the three years that P.F.I. had been investigating and taking tours in the Gaol, they certainly had not had a problem with this door previously. Jeff, who had also been videotaping an interview with Michael for the records, frowned at his camera. A battery that had been reading 174mins had suddenly dropped to 80mins of remaining power. All they could do was shrug: after all what could be done about it? All they had was a banging door and a dying battery – just one of those quirky moments that were common in this remarkable building.

But this was to be a night of quirky events, all uncatchable, as if the Gaol was teasing them that night. Patrick and Jeff, sitting on the steps in 'B' Wing, started to hear whistling which lasted for a few seconds. Upon asking the other two investigators who were standing close to the same area – only above on the second level – they were told the others had not heard a thing. Unusual yet again, since it had been so loud it should have been heard throughout the building. Patrick was quick to point out that it seemed to have started the moment that Jeff had put his video camera on 'pause' and when he had repositioned himself and turned it back on the whistling had stopped as suddenly as it started. Not an uncommon event when trying to capture such phenomena. Other noises followed, all subtle, and all again unable to be caught. All stopped as suddenly as they started once an investigator's curiosity had been aroused enough to take a look.

Finally it was time to leave the Gaol in peace once more, and Patrick and Jeff returned to the caretaker's room to pack up the equipment. Having finished up in the New Building, Michael walked back into the tunnel to join up with the rest of the team. As he was approaching the end he suddenly felt uncomfortable and turned around half expecting to see something in the tunnel with him: what he observed instead was the door slowly closing behind him. It paused momentarily a few centimetres from the doorframe before suddenly slamming shut so loudly that once again Patrick and Jeff came out to see what had made the noise.

Although the night had not been productive on evidence, the Gaol had certainly made her presence felt enough, especially to the new P.F.I. recruit, Michael. Was she welcoming the new boy? It became known over time that the new tour recruits or members quite often seemingly would be picked upon. On my tours there is always a sigh of relief when a new backup person starts and the second-newest passes over the role at last.

—ooo—

The year 2005 rolled over to 2006 and it wasn't until April that we held our first investigation at the Gaol. Michael had only stayed with us for a brief time his interest, like many others, waning once the reality of the work began to sink in.

By now, though, two new members had joined us, Anna and Johanna. These ladies had come to us at separate times: Anna being introduced to the team by a mutual friend, and Johanna through our website. That April night was to be their first night in the Gaol.

The activity seemingly began almost immediately: maybe the new people caught their curiosity. Having set up security cameras and our trigger device, Jeff had settled himself into one of the yards with Johanna. Sitting quietly, he suddenly jumped; something or somebody had just touched him on the shoulder. He turned fully expecting it to be Johanna, only to find her still seated across the yard. Nobody was close by, yet he was sure that he had felt this firm touch, and even felt the jacket press down. Taking a deep breathe he resumed taking pictures with his camera – only to be interrupted again by banging noises coming from one of the cells. Jumping to his feet, he made his way over to the cell but found it empty and now very still. A light flashed red in his hand, drawing his attention down to the EMF [Electro Magnetic Field] meter he was holding: strangely it was spiking at 1.5mG. But soon events calmed down once more in this yard. Jeff waited, but nothing more was to reveal itself and soon it was decided to swap positions to another location.

Meanwhile Patrick, Anna and I had entered the Remand Centre and walked through into the cellblock area. I was positioning myself, and directing where the others should sit, when Anna turned to me: "Do you smell that?"

Patrick and Anna walked over to where I was standing centrally in the cellblock and sniffed the air. "Burning," Patrick answered, "like a wood with oil/chemical smell intermingled".

"Maybe a train has gone past," I suggested, and we quickly moved down to the bottom entrance. A railway yard and track sit directly behind the outer Gaol walls, and freight trains are a common occurrence during the course of the night. However, standing out on the grassy walkway the air was clean with no sign of engine fumes. Besides, the smell had definitely not smelt like diesel. It was an unclean smell, much like burning plastic. Shaking my head we re-entered the Remand Centre and walked back to our position – only to find the clogging smell still present. It would seem that it was only in the dead centre of the block. Upon wandering slightly away the smell seemed to disappear completely. A few moments later it vanished altogether. I jumped as my two-way crackled loudly. Interference of some sort was starting to affect the hand-held device that was still sitting in my pocket. The noise became more insistent, eventually causing me to switch it off altogether. With the incident now over, we settled ourselves down to monitor the block quietly.

"That's odd," Jeff looked at the radio that was now in his hand and tried to puzzle out why it was making such a terrible noise that sounded like birds screeching through static. Thinking I may be trying to contact him, he tried to radio me but there was no reply. What he found most unusual, however, was the cold chill that had brushed passed him as the radio had started to play up. After a few moments the radio settled down, and sliding it back into his pocket Jeff continued to observe his new position in 'A' Wing. After leaving the yard they had been monitoring, Jeff and Johanna had headed over to the New Building. Once inside they had split up: Johanna settling in 'C' Wing, and Jeff sitting himself by the condemned cells in 'A' Wing.

As Jeff checked through the viewfinder of the video camera that stood before him on the tripod, he shivered. A cold chill had just passed by once more, and yet again the two-way began to crackle loudly. An uncomfortable feeling accompanied the cold chill making him feel uneasy, but remaining calm he tried to rationalize it nonetheless: "It was probably just coincidence… and the cold chill? More than likely just a breeze coming from one of the windows in the condemned cells, nothing more."

The incident that happened ten minutes later was a little harder to explain. Sitting quietly on his own in the dark, the cold chill made its presence felt yet again, and the radio in his pocket screamed out as if issuing forth a warning. Reaching for the two-way Jeff paused as another sound appeared to be coming from the darkened cell to his side. He listened closer… yes there it was… the unmistakable chatter of two men having a conversation. The sounds were muffled and the words unclear – as if they were in another room – but he definitely described it as sounds of conversation. Jeff by this stage was starting to feel extremely uncomfortable and shone the torch through into the cell, only to find it empty. The conversation stopped dead as the beam bounced its way around the cell walls. Reaching for his video camera he paused to look at it: something wasn't right, it had stopped working! Strangely, the power was still there but all functions on the camera had ceased to respond. As he pressed each button in turn, a feeling started to creep over him… things were feeling very wrong!

"What the…" Jeff leapt up, nearly toppling the deck chair over in which he had been seated. Somebody had touched him on his left shoulder, the shoulder that had been nearest the cell. It wasn't so much the touch that had startled him, but the feel of the touch. A very cold hand had seemingly bypassed his jacket and shirt altogether and firmly pressed directly onto the skin of his shoulder. Standing his ground, Jeff swung the torch back once more, desperately flashing it around in the hope it would reveal another team member – or anything that would explain the strange sensation. Still nothing!

BLEEP!

The noise made Jeff spin around: the camera was now viewing the Wing as if nothing had happened. Tentatively he pressed the buttons: yes, they were working once again. The moment seemed to have passed and peace once more fell over the block. Jeff felt that although it had not appeared to him to be an aggressive gesture, he still needed to have a break and maybe confer with another investigator about what had just happened. Moving into 'B' Wing he joined Johanna and sat down on the metal steps.

Ghosts of the Past

"Can you feel that?" Twenty minutes had passed and Jeff was again feeling a chill around him. This time, however, it appeared to fill the whole area, and was not just a quick passing breeze. It was becoming almost refrigerated and he began to shiver.

"Yes," Johanna called back from the end of 'B' Wing, "it is suddenly feeling much colder in here".

Grabbing for the temperature meter he quickly read the numbers on the display. Strange, the ambient temperature was still reading 16°C and yet it was feeling much colder. Jeff was almost expecting to see his breath form a cloud as it felt like the chill of a cold winter's night. It would be interesting to note here, though, that often when investigators appear to be feeling dramatic temperature changes, nothing registers on the equipment. Often in these cases the EMF is not affected either. Could this possibly be an indication that these sensations are originating from the minds of the people experiencing it and maybe not an external physical effect? – or could it be that the energy affects our body heat?

Soon the temperature started to normalise again and the area seemed to become calm once more. A short time later the investigation for that night was completed without further event.

It was the next day that Jeff as usual reported to the Manager. She was very interested in the burning incident. We learnt how on 30th December 1983 riots broke out in the Remand Centre involving 86 prisoners and nine Correctional Service officers. According to newspaper articles of the day, one of the inmates had become a little too friendly with a female visitor and he had been punished for it. Other prisoners there objected to this and on getting no satisfaction from the prison guards, staged a sit-in. The situation deteriorated with violence flaring up later in the evening at around 9–9.30 pm. (I mention the time because it is interesting to note that it was the same time that we had experienced the strong smell of burning in the Remand Centre.) Furniture and fittings had been dragged out of cells and piled in strategic areas of the building, then fires were lit to keep the guards at bay. Star-Force and the dogs were called in and the riot was quelled at around eleven o'clock that night – but not before 25 of the 40 cells had suffered damage. It was claimed to be the worst riots in the Gaol's history.

Although the dates don't match as to when the team experienced the burning smell, the time of night does. It probably would be assumptive to make the connection that maybe what we experienced could be no more than a residual

Winds of Change

event of something that happened many years ago. But it was curious to note, nonetheless.

—oOo—

More examples of possible residual events were again experienced on the next investigation we held in the Gaol.

It was now June 2006 and the winds of change were starting to blow. At the time we weren't to know it; but this was going to be our last official investigation of the Adelaide Gaol for quite some time.

Only four investigators turned up this night. Teaming up into pairs, it was Jeff and Patrick who positioned themselves in the New Building. Jeff again settled himself in 'A' Wing and sat patiently monitoring.

'Is that my imagination?' Jeff thought to himself, studying the mannequins up on the top floor. A creaking noise had diverted his attention to the above area. Now he was convinced that he could see the mannequin of the condemned prisoner rocking slowly back and forth. He questioned what he was seeing: was

Mannequins on the top floor of 'A' Wing.

this just an optical illusion? As he stood puzzling over this, he continued to watch the slow rocking motion before it stilled once more. Jeff continued to gaze up at the display, but eventually his attention drifted elsewhere as there was no more apparent movement to be observed.

It was soon time for a break. Radioing through to Anna and Johanna, Jeff told them he would meet back in the Sallyport. It was as he stepped outside the New Building's threshold that a loud wooden-sounding crash echoed through the building making him spin round. Hurrying back in, he expected to see part of the ceiling to have collapsed. As he wandered around scanning the area, there appeared to be nothing amiss. There was no rubble on the floor, no bits hanging from the ceiling; in fact nothing at all to indicate where the crash had originated from. All was now silent. Standing at the end of 'A' Wing he glanced up and pondered on whether, in fact, what he had heard was the sound a trapdoor opening would have made. The Manager confirmed it would have made one hell of a noise as it dropped down, so allowing the prisoner to fall through. A sound from long ago, just echoing through time and space? Interestingly the same noise has been heard elsewhere in the Gaol, and often on tours. It has been described again as a dull wooden crash – but this time coming from that more infamous building that also holds a trapdoor in its heart: the structure now known as the Hanging Tower.

Hanging Tower, gallows and trapdoor.

Finally those winds of change blew hard, and P.F.I. reached a crisis point.

"I am leaving the team," announced Jeff as he stood in the Sallyport a week or so later, "I just don't have the time and I want to branch out into the UFO field".

"You can't," Anna exclaimed in a panic, "I just joined, what will happen now?"

Jeff nodded across at me, "Well Alison is still here".

I looked at them all doubtfully. I had been sick for sometime now. My ability for report writing and all-night investigations had diminished gradually as massive headaches were taking their toll five days out of seven. They had become so severe that they had even forced me to shut down my own horse therapy business. It was a condition the doctors were proving unable to get to the bottom of. Although the new tablets they had put me on had brought the crashing pain to a halt, they also left me feeling tired and dulled in my thinking. I shook my head slowly and looked at them again, "I really don't know…"

Anna looked almost desperate and I didn't have the heart to let her down, or any of the others, who I knew wanted the team to continue. Sighing heavily I nodded ,"OK, I will keep it going for the time being and see how we go". Anna's face lit up, her relief readily apparent.

And so it was that crisis was averted for the time being. But it would seem that those winds of change were not finished with our involvement with the Gaol quite yet, and one more development was starting to blow in.

Ghosts of the Past

Walkway at the side of New Building

Chapter 8
Worries and Workshops

"Standing in the Remand Centre watching the video and photos, I felt a cold feeling across my back and neck, then a breeze seemed to move my hair. It then happened to my friend who had just witnessed my hair move."

(Ruby, Ghost Tour)

THE FULL activities of P.F.I. were on hold for the time being whilst I thought about ways to move it forward; the Ghost Tours continued and Jeff remained to help conduct these along with myself. In reality this was just a stalling period to see if I could take up the reins fully on my own.

Winter was now creeping in once again and this particular Ghost Tour proved to be a problematic one before we even set out. It was the monthly public tour and a lady had booked in with two children. The problem became more apparent when she turned up with not two, but with five, the oldest being approximately ten and the youngest looked no older than five or six. They all stood there excited about the prospect of seeing a ghost. The mother had brought them along as part of her daughter's birthday sleepover. I looked at the expressions of eagerness on their faces, then glanced quickly at the rest of the tour group – who didn't look quite so thrilled. They had obviously already sensed our apprehension that with children so young present we would need to be careful about the stories we told. We certainly felt just as unhappy as the group, and silently agreed that these children were far too young for such a tour.

I motioned to Jeff and we quickly stepped outside away from the tour: "What if I take them on their own and give them the Playschool version?" I muttered.

"That would probably work better," Jeff agreed, glancing back at the tour, "besides there aren't too many, I should be able to cope on my own".

Ghosts of the Past

And so it was that I gathered up the mother and the children and proceeded to move them away from the main tour. Things went well as I told them all about the characters who possibly still called the Gaol their home. All the while I was reassuring them that IF ghosts did exist that they were only people; and just because they had passed away did not automatically make them evil monsters. I also reassured them that in my twenty years of investigating I had never known anybody to have been hurt by a 'ghost', and that generally they were quite harmless. Although scared and clutching one another, they still managed to remain calm.

"One last building," I told them brightly as we walked through the gloomy entrance of 'C' Wing and into the large internal cell block of the New Building. I took up my usual position on the third step of the old metal staircase and smiled down at them reassuringly. Their unease had obviously just doubled as they found themselves now in this silent forbidding building. I watched them nervously glancing around, as they weighed up how far it was to the nearest exit if there was a need to bolt.

"Welcome to our most active building," I smiled again at them before adding, "but don't worry, the man who lives in here is a lovely man". I flashed my torch to the top of the stairs behind me to show them where he was normally seen. I shared with them the story of the electrician who had been putting up lights for a party, only to find a face smiling back at him through the bars – all the while putting an emphasis on the 'smiling' part of the story. Still they clutched each other tighter.

"It's OK," I reassured them again, "he would do NOTHING to scare you…" I broke off from my sentence as a now familiar sound was heard from the top gantry. The sound of sturdy boots… a sound that was steadily getting closer to the top of the stairs. The incident with the two documentary makers crossed my mind quickly, and how the footsteps had come down the stairs.

'Oh God, not now,' I implored quietly in my mind. 'Please, not now!'

I breathed a sigh of relief as they stopped by the upper office gate and went silent once more. Turning back to the children smiling, ready to reassure them again, I realised it was too late. The kids were now inseparable, with heads buried into each others shoulders, and the unhappy sounds of mewling and sobbing were clearly heard as I smiled at them weakly.

"Wow!" I said brightly, whilst glaring back up the stairs: "Do you know how lucky you are? He must really like you!"

The children, however, were not buying it; and there was nothing left to do but gather them up and carefully guide them back to the shop area to settle them down. Ten minutes later Jeff entered the New Building with his tour, but nothing of interest had happened. All was quiet for his group. Why it would perform for some little kids and terrify them, but not for the normal tours, I have no idea – but I know the names I had for 'him' that night weren't so nice!

—ooo—

Autumn of 2006 arrived and Anna decided that the Gaol would be a great place for her son to celebrate his 13th birthday. Twenty-one people arrived for the night which consisted mainly of her son's friends and six supervising adults. Jeff was chosen to be their tour guide for the night. The following events were written by Anna herself:

"This is a story of our sleepover at the Adelaide Gaol for my son Dayton's 13th. We began at 5.00pm and there were twenty-one of us, six being adults. At 7.00pm we headed for our tour. It was on completion of our tour that things started to happen. The tour ended and we headed back to the dormitory to watch a video and listen to EVP [Electronic Voice Phenomena] material. As we were about to listen to the EVP we had a gentleman who was also there with his wife for his birthday – which funnily enough is on the same day as my son's – shout out: 'Who turned the fan on?' There was a large free-standing fan in the room which sits on a stand. The unit was switched on at the wall, but to turn on the fan you had to flick the switch. Well, I can tell you there were a few sceptics with no way of explaining that one, and I myself was over the moon to get a strange, possibly paranormal, happening.

"We had a few more strange happenings on our sleepless sleepover. When the boys had arrived they had picked the second room to sleep in; but all of a sudden they came running out saying that two of the boys saw an orb and wanted me to go and take pictures. So off I went, with the boys trailing right behind me and grabbing their gear along the way. At least a few of them admitted they were scared. I was acting as the Gaol warden for the night, walking up and down and telling the kids to be quiet. It was as I looked towards the door that I witnessed a dark shadow moving across it before I watched the door open and slam shut again… there was no wind or breeze at the time. Hubby had taken the plunge and decided he would sleep in this area too but was woken by the bang. Now the weirdest thing of the night was this: the boys had their mobiles and were phoning each other, and the boy that was the most frightened had his phone rung by another boy. The already nervous boy told the other to hang up as his phone was ringing and he couldn't answer it. When the other *boy told him he HAD hung up they came running up to the kitchen to find me and gave me his phone. I was pressing all the buttons but couldn't get his phone to stop ringing, and the phone itself just had the phone network on it. We had to actually turn the phone off to eventually stop it.*

"Well this is our story of the Adelaide Gaol sleepover. There are so many stories that this grand old structure has to tell and many more to come, of that I am sure. If you ever get the chance, make your way to this fascinating historical site with so much history, stories and possibly GHOSTS!"

—000—

As 2007 rolled in, it was decided that maybe the tours could be expanded, and that maybe workshop nights would be a good way of raising money for the Gaol. So Jeff devised an outline for them and ran them with P.F.I. involvement with Anna and myself there to assist on the night. It was worked out that ten members of the public could come and spend a night investigating at the Gaol and have use of P.F.I. equipment and knowledge in the field. They would start with tea and a talk on various aspects of the paranormal and a look at what P.F.I. had experienced and captured in the Gaol on past investigations. This was to be followed by a Ghost Tour before splitting into two teams and settling in for a night of work and fun.

By April, the first workshop was ready to go and eleven excited people turned up. It wasn't far into the night before the Gaol started to perform for them. I had taken half the group, backed up by Anna, into the New Building; whilst Jeff and his group went into Yard 2. He decided to place three of the ladies into the Recreation Room that divides Yards 2 and 3, and it was there that they sat nervously adjusting to the darkness on their own. Jeff smiled and reassured them that he was just outside in Yard 2 should they have a problem.

Standing over near the old kitchen, Jeff took a moment to have a breather: it had been a long night, and so far he had done most of the talking, so now he leant against the door and relaxed.

Knock, knock, knock!

Startled, Jeff temporarily jumped back from the door he had been leaning against before taking a closer look. It had sounded like somebody knocking on the door from the inside of the kitchen. This was impossible, he knew, because the floor had collapsed in the kitchen only recently and now the doors were firmly locked for safety reasons. Peering through the old windows nothing was to be seen, and after a while without further incident he shrugged it off and went to see how his small team was doing. It wasn't long after that two other people from the group also heard the rapping on the door.

Meanwhile in Yard 4 my team was working quietly only to be disrupted by the speaker box springing to life. In those days the Gaol had various speaker boxes for visitors to press a button and hear the history of that particular point of interest. We soon found out a natural explanation to this: one of the guests had thought it was a light switch and had turned it on.

"Don't worry, I will go turn it off," volunteered Anna. I nodded and settled back onto the step of the old porta-cabin where I had positioned myself. I watched as Anna disappeared out into the Turning Circle through the far door in the yard.

I glanced up quickly a few moments later as a figure hurried back towards me. Anna had re-entered the yard, and although not running, her pace was certainly accelerated.

'Hello...' I thought to myself, 'something has happened'. As she reached me I soon realised I was right.

The following is Anna's explanation of her experience:

"At 2.45am: We had just moved to Yard 4 when someone turned on the speaker box and I called out to Alison that I was going to turn it off. It was turned on accidentally by one of the investigators who had mistaken it for a light switch. I walked out of the yard and entered the Circle, looking in the direction of the Visitor's Centre. It was then that I saw someone walking towards the VJ room through the glass of the Visitor's Centre. Thinking it was Jeff, I called out, 'Jeff, Jeff is that you?' I had assumed it may have been Jeff going to the toilet so I walked over there to check. As I reached the toilets, I said, 'Hello is there anybody there?' There was no response and nobody near the VJ room and nowhere for them to go.

I headed back to Alison, by now realising that what I had seen was not human as there was nobody in the area. The other investigators from the group all gathered in the Circle area and we discussed what I had just experienced. We got one of the gentlemen to walk in the direction of the toilet. With him being a solid figure, he could be seen very clearly. This was done also to see that if someone was in the toilet, would they be able to hear me if I called out. He was able to hear me very clearly and responded. The figure that I witnessed was also taller. We worked out that he was approximately 6ft (180cm) by getting one of the taller guys in the Group to walk past, and I worked out that he was approximately the size of the figure I saw . The figure was not solid: the best way to describe the figure was that if I looked through a tinted window, it would look blurry. It was a shadow-type figure which appeared to be wearing a brown jumper with a hood on as I couldn't see the head. The brown jumper I would describe as having been washed many times and looked like a light brown. I also noticed that when the figure got closer to the VJ room it appeared to get larger and appeared to light-up…not too bright, but as if he had passed by a light and the light shone through the figure."

Although nothing more happened that night the people were wrapped with their experience, and even though tiredness had now taken them over they were still excitedly comparing notes over breakfast. Anna of course took a special memory home with her that morning.

—ooo—

Word soon got around, and by our second workshop a couple of months later people were clamouring to come on, and we found we had to refuse some so that we could keep it small and more personal.

It was on that first workshop that a girl had arrived and taken part on her own. She had attracted our attention because she had worked quietly, but with a thoroughness and rational thinking that impressive us. She obviously had been equally impressed with the night too, as a few days later she rang Jeff and asked if she could assist with further workshops. Being shorthanded we were more than happy to have her on board. I, however, wanted her there for a different reason: I wanted to observe her further as I could see the makings of a prospective P.F.I. investigator. And so it was that Amy was invited along to our next workshop.

In fact it was Amy who seemed to have the experiences that night. The first subtle experience took place whilst we were still doing the Ghost Tour. Amy had been standing in 'A' Wing when she felt somebody touch the back of her hat in a gentle way. Turning she expected to see a person behind her, but she was fairly much at the rear and nobody in the vicinity would have been able to reach the point where she had felt the touch. Not dwelling on it too much, and putting it down to possible imagination, she moved on.

The tour soon came to an end and the team had split into the usual two groups of five, with Anna and me taking Team One, whilst Jeff teamed up with Amy and took Team Two into Yard 2.

"Do you hear that?" Amy looked across at Jeff, "Piano music?"

Jeff gave a puzzled look and shook his head. He certainly hadn't heard anything. Amy went on to tell him that she had just heard the sound of a piano being played and described it as being old-style playing. Yet again the music had been heard drifting through the ether of the Gaol. Strangely we hadn't been telling the stories of the piano playing on the tours: we were trying to keep them short and to the point, focusing more on the investigation side of it. But the Gaol hadn't finished with Amy just yet.

Exchanging areas, Jeff and Amy took their team and positioned them in the New Building. Wandering up the stairs, Amy walked into the Guard's offices that lay at the top of the stairs where 'Sgt Murphy', as we nicknamed him, was said to be seen frequently. Wandering into one of the rooms she came to a sudden halt. She reached quickly for her hat: the Beanie she was wearing was once more being touched, but this time it felt as if it was physically being moved from side to side with such force that her head was made to keep up with the movement. Quickly she backed out of the room and found Jeff so that he could log the incident. Walking back down the stairs Amy decided to settle herself on the old metal staircase instead, sitting on the bottom step.

"Ohhh!" Amy exclaimed quickly, "my left side has just chilled". She started to rub at her left arm and leg vigorously.

Pulling the laser thermometer out of her pocket, one of our guests hurried over to her and started to compare temperatures of both her left shoulder and knee from her right. Her eyes widened as she showed Amy the measurements. The left shoulder and knee were indeed much colder now then her right. Her surface temperature on the affected areas had dropped to 8–9°C, whilst her right was reading on average around 21°C. So there did seem to have been a physical affect on Amy's body. They took more readings and watched as the temperature slowly normalised to the 21°C that the rest of the body was showing.

"Wow... that's intriguing." Discussing with Amy what she had just experienced, I set my coffee back down on the bench I was leaning against. It had been a long night already, and we were all now taking a break and desperately trying to stay awake by filling up once more with strong caffeine. I started to recount the time that I had been hit by that wall of cold whilst standing in the same area. I could only wonder what the readings would have been like had we taken some with that experience. It was strange, though, that this had happened once more in that same area.

Picking up my gear and motioning to my team, we wearily headed off for the last stakeout, leaving Jeff and his team to finish their coffees. It was whilst his team were mustering up the energy to move, that a strange voice seemed to emanate from the centre of the table. They described it as a muffled male voice with electronic undertones. It lasted for a few seconds then ceased. Everybody just looked at each other as if to say, 'Did you just hear that?'

Jeff thought at first that it may just be one of the other team contacting him on the two-way, so drew it out of his pocket and called them back. The answer was a negative. Nobody from the other team had called through. Besides, all had agreed it had come centrally to them as if from the table itself. This was so real to them that they all briefly checked their mobile phones; and Jeff even checked the CD player, video recorder and anything else he could find in the room that could possibly have been responsible. But nothing. No device had power to it.

Realising after a while that not much else was going to happen, they moved off to complete their investigation – this time without any further incident.

—oOo—

It was still 2007 when, finally, the winds of change took hold at the Gaol. A memo had surfaced stating that they were looking at closing the Gaol down. This is a huge building which needs high maintenance: an expensive prospect for any owner. According to the memo, the government department at the time had decided it was not viable any longer to remain open to the public. This was devastating news to us all, and of course not news that we were going to take lightly. It was a decision that would not just affect our investigation and tour work there, but a decision that cut to the very heart of those who had come to love the Old Girl herself for her architecture and her history.

The volunteers for the Adelaide Gaol Preservation Society (AGPS) rallied together and they did a marvellous job by bringing just how important the Gaol was to the attention of the Minister involved. Discussions were held and the Gaol was saved. The public have much to thank the AGPS members for, as it is their love and passion for this remarkable building that helped to save her.

Worries and Workshops

Naturally changes had to take place. First to be changed was the pulling of the Ghost Tours and the sleepovers. We were told that we could complete the tours that were already booked in, but then their days were finished. New management stepped in and a whole new chapter of the Gaol's history began.

And so it was that we were allowed to complete the third and final workshop. Although it was with heavy hearts that it was conducted, it became an enjoyable and productive night nonetheless.

Again the teams were split into two, with Jeff and Anna this time leading Team One and Amy and myself taking Team Two. Our first port of call was the New Building.

"I might put you in the Solitary Cell at the end there," I said to Amy, as I wandered through contemplating our plan of action.

The Solitary Cells in 'A' Wing are situated on either side of the open doorway

Ghosts of the Past

Amy agreed that it would be a good place to start, and she and another of our lady guests settled themselves on the stark wooden bed within the cell's confining walls.

"Maybe do some EVP work," I suggested, and left to position the rest of my team in other sections of the New Building.

There was a reason that I had chosen this cell for them. An ex-guard who I had met with, and who had loaned me his memoirs of his years spent at the Gaol, had mentioned something of interest in them. I had discovered a paragraph relating to this cell in particular. Apparently, there had been an Aboriginal gentleman in the later workings of the Goal, who would misbehave on a regular basis. This would of course mean time in the Solitary Confinement Cells, or the 'hole', as an ex-prisoner once told me they were known as. If the Aboriginal prisoner knew that he was going into the right-hand cell, it would take two guards to get him in there – he didn't want to go and so would protest all the way. However, if he knew he was going into the left-hand cell, it would take five guards to drag him down there – and he would be kicking and screaming all the way. He appeared genuinely fearful of this cell, and eventually the question was asked: 'Why?' He told of how at night as he lay on the bed, Charles O'Leary would walk through the outer wall and stand over his bed. (Charles O'Leary was one of the men executed and whose remains are buried on the other side of that wall.) However, if it was just an excuse to not be put into solitary, he could have used the same excuse for the opposite cell, as there are a further three people buried there too. He was adamant: it was ONLY in this cell that he would have a dead person visit him during the night.

Once settled, I positioned myself centrally where I could supervise and help with either of the two small groups of people. I could also hear the EVP work that was conducted in the end Solitary Cell.

"Is anybody there?" Amy asked. "When did you die?"

I hesitated before I made my way back down to them. I have always theorised that if ghosts exist and if I was one of them, I would not be so keen to respond to such mundane questions. I personally like to try and interact on a more personal level when experimenting with EVP. If it is true that when we die our personalities continue, then surely we would still like to be talked to on our level with recognition of who we still may be. With this in mind I wandered into the Solitary Cell to join Amy and our guest.

"Why not try a different approach," I suggested. "We know the story told about this cell involves Charles O'Leary, why not talk to him direct?"

As I said the name, 'Charles O'Leary', a distinct chill filled the air around me and I involuntarily shuddered. Amy must have felt it too, as she looked at me and rubbed at her own arms. She nodded her agreement, and smiling I left them to it so I could see how the others were getting on.

Finding all was going well, I stood centrally once more so I could monitor both small groups. It was as I stood there, I listened to Amy playing some of her audio back. I slowly straightened and focused my attention once more on that small little cell. Did I just hear what I thought I heard?

"Can you just play that back?" I asked, now standing in the doorway of their cell once more. "Back to where you are complaining about the cold!"

Amy quickly rewound her tape a short way then pressed the 'play' button, and looked up at me puzzling as to what I thought I had heard. Sure enough there was Amy's voice clearly stating how cold she was.

"Play it back again… and this time listen harder," I encouraged.

"Oh… there's a man's voice there!" she stated, excitement creeping into her voice.

Sure enough you could clearly hear Amy talking about how cold it had become in the cell. Whilst she was still speaking a male voice clearly comes over the top of hers "I'm Soooo Cold!"

What Amy didn't know at the time, was that P.F.I. had been sent such a recording before. A group of ladies had been sleeping the night in the Dormitories. In the early hours of the morning, one of the ladies couldn't sleep so she started to videotape with her camera phone. A male voice is clearly heard: "I'm cold, so cold." Strange, as no males were present that night.

Happy that we may have captured something, we continued our monitoring quietly.

Meanwhile in Yard 4, Jeff's team was having a couple of incidents themselves. Part of Jeff's team had positioned themselves in the oldest cellblock there, which

Ghosts of the Past

The old cell blocks in Yard 4

in the later years had become the canteen/dining area. It is our darkest building and at present contains a Mary Mackillop display.

One of the men on Jeff's team hesitated: "Did you just see that?" He looked quickly across at Jeff who was standing close by.

Jeff confirmed that he had just seen a shadowy black form moving across the room. Both described it as being very dark – in fact darker than this room was at the time – and without any discernable features. It appeared to be the size and shape of a fully-grown man. (This would not be the last time this figure was seen: I was to be witness to it some years later.)

But it was as they swapped their positions in the New Building that things started to become more interesting for them.

Settling themselves in positions around the New Building, Jeff decided to videotape in one of the Wings. Moving towards the centre he pointed his camera up and a sudden movement caught his attention. A dark shadowy form was moving along the top gantry towards the window at the end of the wing. He watched and attempted to videotape, but as he did so it disappeared out of sight – only to reappear again and stop by the same window. The figure was apparent on and off for three or four minutes. Jeff wasn't the only person witnessing this event: one of the guest investigators was starting to get fairly nervous as he too had witnessed the same figure. This man had been positioned at the top of the stairs and was sitting comfortably monitoring the area when he too had seen movement. A shadowy form appeared to be walking towards him, making him feel uneasy. But still he held his nerve and watched until he lost sight of it. He too described this form as being the height of an average male with no distinctive features to be noted.

It was not long before one of the other guest investigators who had moved down further into the Wing, also saw this figure. This time the guest called out to the figure with a comment; then became concerned when the shadowy figure appeared to adopt a more aggressive stance and could clearly be seen stopping and putting hands on hips before disappearing. This was too much for this particular guest and he hastily left the area.

Regrouping at the foot of the stairs, discussing what had just been seen, they paused in their conversation as a loud noise was heard from up above. They all described it as sounding like a large belch. Surprised, they looked at each other, and then another noise started to spook the guests. At first it was whispering conversation, closely followed by a sound that was metal-on-metal – almost as if something metallic was knocking on the above railings. One of the girls started to feel uneasy and was ready then and there to leave.

Things soon calmed down in there once more, and it seemed the moment was over.

And so the end of the workshop came too soon, and we found ourselves bidding people goodbye. It was with a heavy heart that we did this, as we were more than aware of the finality of this workshop. We knew the Gaol that we had become so fond of, and our freedom to investigate and take tours, had just come to an end. At this point it cannot be stated enough just how easy it is to fall in love with this old building, its history and whatever may still dwell within its walls.

A few weeks later, new management stepped in and a whole new chapter for the Gaol was about to begin.

The hangman's noose.

Chapter 9
A New Beginning

"I saw a figure of a man standing on the second storey of 'A' Wing with an old suit on. Three of us then heard footsteps and the covers of the peepholes moving. We also heard coughing and a figure upstairs was seen to be running real fast."
(Sally, Self Guided Ghost Tour)

WE'VE agreed to bring the Ghost Tours back, the new management told us one day, "but there have to be rules set in place".

This was such fantastic news for us, we were happy to comply with any rules imposed. For a year now, although I had remained as a volunteer, I really hadn't had much to do with the Gaol and I sorely missed her. The thought of being able to guide tours once more through her walls was a joy to hear.

Rules were put in place to keep people safe. Lights now had to be turned on. There would be no scaring the guests, and unsafe areas had to be pointed out. It was such a relief to have the tours reinstated, that we were more than willing to comply. Deep down we knew there would be no investigation work allowed: but it was a start and it enabled us back into her interior at least.

Although day tours had continued and the public were allowed to stroll through the Gaol at their leisure, all possible paranormal-related activity had appeared to decrease during the absence of night functions. It was almost as if the lack of energy from the visitors also caused apathy in the phenomena as well. Even daytime experiences appeared to reduce. Upon reinstating the tours, things changed once more.

—ooo—

"Welcome to the Old Adelaide Gaol," I smiled at the expectant crowd that were now gathered around me. "We have to cover a few rules," I continued enthusiastically – after all I was feeling good to be back in action.

Ghosts of the Past

It was at this point that a girl on the tour started to look agitated. I remember glancing at her and thinking how strange it was as I hadn't even started with the 'ghost' stories. 'Maybe she is just the nervous type,' I thought and continued with the rules. But her demeanour became more worrying and soon she spoke up. She was starting to feel hot, and a strong feeling of nausea had come over her. My backup that night quickly stepped in and escorted her outside into the car park, where she was offered a drink. Meanwhile the stories began and the tour kicked off. After making it clear that we could NOT promise a 'ghost' for them tonight, I went on to explain to the crowd what it was that they may experience. The biggest problem we have is that people expect to see ghosts running around on every tour. As one can imagine, this would be unrealistic: the paranormal just does not perform like a circus animal on request. If it did, it would make my job MUCH easier! If we could promise this, our car park would be overflowing daily – both with the sceptics and believers alike – and our beloved Gaol would not be in such disrepair. I have always maintained that if the phenomena were happening so often, then there would be no need for hundreds of groups around the world to research it: we would all be seeing it daily.

With this in mind, we left the shop and entered the Sallyport, just as the girl stepped back through into the Gaol, obviously feeling much better, and the tour continued without incident.

The entrance to the Gaol is through the Sallyport. The guards' office can be seen inside.

A New Beginning

However, this was not going to be the last time we had somebody get sick. Two weeks later, once again as I was explaining the rules, a lady in the crowd started to become agitated, started to pale and asked to be excused as she was feeling sick. At this point I was hoping it wasn't a reflection of my tour! I watched as my backup yet again escorted the person out and offered them a drink. Once more the person returned, feeling well and back to normal, and once more continued the tour without any further incident.

It was on a third tour that we had another re-occurrence. This time I was not rostered on as the guide, but tagging along anyway. Standing by the shop door, I switched the lights off for the tour and stood listening to the other guide telling her tales when a noise drew my attention to the Sallyport. Footsteps, clear and loud walked passed. 'But all the tour are in there,' I thought to myself curiously, but decided I should check it out anyway. Quietly slipping out into the Sallyport, so as not to disturb the tour, I found it to be empty. I walked quickly out into the main body of the Gaol, only to find no evidence of anybody having been there either.

"Alison!!!!" Penny's shout for help echoed through the Sallyport to me, and I hurried back to the shop.

Penny pointed to a young man who was now leaning against one of the display cupboards, looking decidedly pale. She didn't need to explain what was wrong as I had seen it twice before. Relieved it was not just my tour that was causing people to feel sick, I quickly walked him out of the area and sat him down at the Visitor's Centre and offered him some water. He sat on the step, head hung low, and took deep breaths.

"It was strange," he said to my questioning, "I was feeling well one minute, then suddenly hot and sweaty the next… then this deep pit-of-the-stomach nausea developed". Again he took another mouthful of water and went quiet, whilst he fought to keep the nausea from developing further. Soon he nodded that he was feeling better and stood up. Indeed the colour had returned to his face and he smiled once more. I guided him back to his tour and he felt fine for the rest of the duration.

So now we appeared to have a whole new phenomena happening… one that only seemed to be happening now tours had been newly established. There was one more major incident like this but, like many things that happen in the Gaol, this particular phenomenon soon died down, and although we still get the odd person being mysteriously hit by this illness, it is not a common occurrence anymore.

—000—

The black shadowy form also seemed to be making regular appearances around the Gaol, especially in Yard 4: one of which I was to experience myself. This was the same yard where, on our last workshop, we had witnessed the shadowy form in the dining/cell block.

"OK…Yard 4…" I started, "When we first came into the Gaol, we were told that…" It was at this point that I broke off from my usual spiel to stare quizzically into the gloom. Momentarily I was unaware of the expectant tour group gathered around me, and stared passed them trying to focus on the furthest corner of the yard where the double-storey cellblock stood. Movement had caught my eye. I was sure I had just seen the dark figure of a man walking between four of the archways before losing sight of him. Only this form was so dark that there had been no discernable features at all. Shaking my head slowly, my attention was suddenly brought back to the tour – who were now nervously looking around, wondering why I had stopped talking mid-sentence, and instead had stood with my mouth open.

Yard 4 'C' Block

A New Beginning

"You are putting this on..." one woman exclaimed nervously, trying to see what it was I was looking at.

"Sorry," I said, shaking my head and smiling once more at the crowd. "Don't worry about it... just a trick of light," I reassured them before continuing with the stories. I have always had a problem with declaring to the tours that I had just seen something:-it would seem as though I had a vested interest in this, and so it would not be believed anyway. This occasion was no different, and I proceeded with the tour without explaining what I had seen.

As the tour was leaving, two men came up to me in the shop area, where I was now packing things away, and asked if they could have a word.

"We know what you saw!" one leant forward and tentatively looked around to make sure others weren't listening. "It was a shadowy figure of a man in the far archways," he continued. The other man stood slightly back nodding in agreement. It appeared that they too had witnessed it: only they had seen it not just once, but twice, and described it exactly the way I had observed it. Strange, as I had never let on what it was that I had seen whilst on the tour itself.

It was only a couple of weeks later that it was witnessed once more. A lady gasped as I started my stories about the yard, and pointed over to the bottom archways opposite. "I just saw a dark figure of a man," she exclaimed nervously. I smiled and proceeded to explain what had happened only a couple of weeks earlier.

—o0o—

There has been a constant stream of incidents experienced on the tours. Sometimes they are only subtle: such as air blowing over faces, the stroking of hair, or feelings of extreme discomfort. A lot, of course, can be put down to over-active imaginations – we are on 'ghost' tours after all – but one incident did stand out recently. I had nearly finished the tour; typically without any incident at all. Our final stop was 'A' Wing, and as the crowd was positioned under the old trap door where 21 people ended their lives, I began to discuss the Solitary Confinement Cells on either side.

"I am sorry but you will have to wait in there..." I told a rather burly gentleman who had just slipped past the door I was holding and had disappeared into the cell. I was in the flow of telling the stories of how the cell was used, and I was not going to stop now just so I could wait for him to come back out. No...he could wait until I reopened the doors! And so it was I shut the first door of Solitary and then demonstrated the shutting of the second door.

"…and they could scream and shout to their hearts content," I smiled, "nobody will be able to hear them".

With that I proceeded to reopen the doors. First the outer door. Then as I reached to open the inner door it crashed open violently, the force hurling me back against the wall. The crowd gasped in surprise and shrunk closer together as the burly gentleman flew out of the cell as if the Devil himself was on his tail.

Recovering myself, I looked across at the now shaking man who had paled considerably. "Are you OK?" I asked painfully, as my arm was beginning to throb where the door had made contact, "what happened in there?"

Solitary confinement cell showing double door.

The gentleman glanced sheepishly around and told me he would tell me later and in a more private setting. I nodded and turned back to the crowd… the show must go on, and I began to wind up with the last stories of the night.

Arriving back at the shop, I was aware of the gentleman hanging patiently in the background as the rest of the tour bought their souvenirs and said their goodbyes. Once the throng had thanked me and left, he stepped forward and explained what had happened.

"I was in the cell," he began, "and you were shutting the doors." He hesitated momentarily and I encouraged him to continue. "Well… as I was in there on my own I could hear your voice, though muffled."

"Yes, they aren't too soundproof now," I confirmed.

Ignoring this he continued: "I was taking a photograph when I heard another voice… a male voice that came from behind me and was in the cell with me."

"Could you tell what it was saying?" I asked, half expecting him to tell me that it was muffled, much like the voices normally reported around the Gaol.

"Yes," he said, slowly nodding his head, "it was very clear… it said GET OUT!"

Well he had certainly taken that advice on board… the bruise that would no doubt be showing on my arm the next day would vouch for that! We chatted some more and I watched as he left the Gaol, still shaken. I couldn't help but feel slightly jealous that he would be going home and taking a great experience with him.

Ghosts of the Past

Adelaide Gaol and her garden.

Chapter 10
Back at Last

"As I walked into the Remand Centre Cell Block, I saw a ball of green light move across the room, zigzagging from side to side and back. It was a bit like a laser, but much bigger and very green."
(Christy, Ghost Tour)

DO YOU mind if I ask something? I stood waiting patiently for Peter's full attention before continuing.

Two years had now passed since the changes came into place. A new Office Manager and Projects Manager had been positioned there, and they had soon grown as fond of the place as the volunteers. This had made our relationships between the Government Department and the Adelaide Gaol Preservation Society (AGPS) much easier, with co-operation between the two strengthening. Our initial fears proved unfounded and the Gaol had now moved forward in a positive way. On top of the working relationship, I had also come to enjoy the private chats and jokes with these two men. I shared a love of photography with one; and a love of the same TV show with another.

But again, life changes and new chapters begin. The wonderful two years of working with these gentlemen were now drawing to a close as their contracts finished and it was time for them to move on. So it was that it was now or never that I approached the last remaining Manager and asked the question outright…

"Would it be possible to let P.F.I. back in to officially investigate once more?"

"Alison, I really can't see a problem with this," Peter agreed – after all, it could only benefit the tours if we were able to gather more data to add to the stories, so keeping them fresh. "I will also write you a letter of introduction and recommendation for future replacements," he added.

I will always be grateful to Peter for this. It was certainly a gift that he left for us and it helped open many more doors.

Ghosts of the Past

We were back! This time it was with a new team, new methods and renewed enthusiasm.

In the early days of our investigations our methods were different and, we will admit, were possibly sloppy. Over the years we evolved our techniques, and learnt from our mistakes. We now had a chance to put these new methods into place, and to commence with experiments and work that were omitted in the earlier investigations.

It was agreed that we would only use those P.F.I. members who were also volunteers at the Gaol. This included Anna and myself, and a new team member who had joined us called Spilios (or Spils, for short). Fortunately, a few weeks earlier he had also joined as a volunteer and was helping me as backup to my Ghost Tours. Spilios was an interesting man – and even more interesting was the story of how he came to be in P.F.I.

"Sorry to ring so early…" came an excited voice at the other end of the phone.

I looked at the clock on my computer that informed me it was still only 8 o'clock on a Sunday morning. 'Who on earth rings at this time,' I thought to myself. Fortunately I am an early riser and had been awake since around 6 am and the early morning coffee had already kicked in. At least I would be able to hold a conversation now.

The gentleman introduced himself as Spilios, and his excitement was obvious as he continued to tell me why he had rung. He had apparently caught an EVP (Electronic Voice Phenomena) in one of our cemeteries the night before, and as it had been his first he couldn't wait to share it with somebody. Eagerly he wanted my thoughts, and offered to send a copy of the EVP to me. Soon after, Spilios was invited to join P.F.I. which he readily agreed to, and now is very much an important part of the team.

Spils also offered to be a volunteer at the Gaol and presently is also one of the backups there. It was on one of these tours that he was to have his first experience.

"Go on, ask," Spils grinned looking across at Debbie Jackson, my backup for the night, and myself. We stood shaking our heads in response.

"You ask!" Debbie suggested back.

Spils – having heard the stories of the keys being locked in the shop and of the footsteps on the stairs after I had asked for something to happen – was eager for us to ask one more time. He desperately wanted to experience something paranormal for himself.

"OK, I will." Looking around at empty space, he spoke up, "Come on Guys… do something!"

Laughing, Debbie and I pointed at Spils and looked around, "Remember guys, it was him that said that, NOT us!" we spoke in unison.

With that the tour arrived and we headed out. The tour itself was quiet that night with nothing to report. It would seem that nothing had listened to Spils' request, and he was fairly disappointed as we waved the tour goodbye and shut the large main doors behind them. At this stage we had only been given permission to hang back for a short time to investigate, but we took full advantage of this and sat around doing a small amount of EVP work in the Remand Centre. Again, nothing eventuated so we decided to call it a night and proceeded to lock up.

As we stepped out of the Remand and into the Turning Circle, we paused and looked at each other. Were those footsteps we just heard? They seemed to have come from the Visitor's Centre, but as we looked into the gloom there was nothing to be seen. We listened momentarily; but all was silent once more and we moved on to the New Building. I followed Debbie into the Tunnel, laughing and joking. I looked back at Spils to observe his reaction to our friendly little dig at him, but instead watched as he blanched and his jaw dropped before uttering, "What the….?"

Realising something was very wrong, and that it obviously wasn't my off-hand comment, I brusquely walked back towards him. His attention was focused towards the Visitor's Centre once more. Shaking his head in disbelief he told how, as he had been about to enter the Tunnel, he had felt the need to turn and have one last look at this building. As he glanced back he had seen a dark figure standing at one of the windows observing us as we moved away. It was there only momentarily before disappearing in front of him. He related that he had seen no features at all: just the dark form of a man standing, silently watching.

"Damn it," I thought out loud, "we may have another intruder!" There was only one thing for it, we would have to go check it out and see if somebody was hiding in there. We knew they had nowhere to go as all yard doors were now

Ghosts of the Past

firmly locked, leaving no escape for the possible intruder. Walking hesitantly back over to the Visitor's Centre – more so because we were nervous of a possible violent living person than anything dead – we nudged Spils into taking a closer look inside. After all he was the only male there, we rationalized, and more capable of handling trouble if it happened.

"We will be right here watching your back," I reassured him, smiling from a distance and waving him forward.

Cementing his place on the team at that very moment for bravery, Spils stepped into the darkened Visitor's Centre and shone his torch around the outer section. The beam fell on empty space, with nobody to be seen. I suggested he move round into the prisoner section in case the intruder was hiding there, which he did. Still emptiness greeted him: all that was to be seen now were the stools – vacated long ago – that prisoners once sat on whilst they met with their friends and relatives. Shaking his head he moved confidently out into the Turning Circle once more, just to double check that the person wasn't now hiding out there. It was then that he became unnerved and soon rejoined Debbie and me. It was as he had moved out into the Circle that footsteps were heard... footsteps from an unseen person stepping towards him. This time, now convinced this was no living person so now feeling much safer, all three of us dashed forward for a closer inspection. But, as

The Visitor's Centre

usual, after attracting attention, it went quiet and nothing more was to be heard. It appeared that Spils had been granted his wish: the Newbie had been broken in at last. Debbie, who had been our previous new backup, was more then happy to hand Spils that torch!

—ooo—

Not long after that we started to resume full investigations, going in on nights when there were no tours to be done. It was now late 2009.

One thing we had been doing over time, despite the lack of investigations, was leaving voice recorders in the New Building as we conducted the tours elsewhere. Many times we had captured sounds and noises that were unusual, but which could have been anything at the end of the day. There had been one particular recording, however, that had made us very curious. A familiar sound had been captured: familiar because I had heard it many times in my late teens and early twenties. It sounded very much like the game of Eight Balls being played. There was a distinct 'clack' of the white ball; a pause, and then a gentle hit and spread of the balls at the far end of a table. Having spent many a night in the local pubs playing Eight Balls, I recognized the sound straight away. But we felt we still needed to confirm this noise as I was not 100% convinced at this stage. So it was that Spils and I returned to the Gaol a week after the sound was captured, armed with a pool cue and a set of pool balls.

If you read the transcript of the interview with the former guard, Andrew, you will remember that the pool table used to be located in the New Building during the 1980s. You will also remember that it spooked one guard on night duty after he had heard it being played in the middle of the night – only to find nobody there to play it (see Chapter 1).

The pool table itself still exists at the Gaol, but is now located in the recreation room. When we uncovered it that night, although the felt had deteriorated, it was still useable enough for the experiment. At this stage all we wanted to do was to create the sounds and compare – and maybe even find out what shot was taken. It was soon discovered that indeed the sounds were near identical: the first sound had been a ball-on-ball, much as if a shot was being lined up. The soft sound of spreading balls at the end of the recording appeared to be caused by that second ball rebounding off the side and gently contacting the grouped balls at the far end. (The full experiment can be found on the Paranormal Field Investigator website.)

Ghosts of the Past

Full moon through the Sallyport

Chapter 11
A New Chapter in Experiments

"In the Sallyport, I heard a couple of men talking loudly and then after the doctors/dentist room, my left hand froze. It was a lot colder than my right hand and I couldn't warm up this hand. It continued throughout the tour and began to ache too."
                                                    (Megan, Ghost Tour)

AND now we come to a more controversial experiment that we have been conducting in the Gaol: and one that I hesitate to write about for risk of losing any shred of credibility we may have worked hard for over the years. But I think it is curious and worth a mention – but for nothing more than story value.

PLEASE NOTE: The following should be taken as entertainment only; NOT as hard evidence, as the method it was captured with and all results have to be seen as tainted.

With Spils, came a new idea – one that I was reluctant to even consider – and I had made my views very clear on our forum of just what I thought about the device that Spils now held in his hand.

"The Ghost Box?" I sneered at the small white radio he held out to show me. "You have to be kidding me, right?"

Spils agreed with my thoughts that technically it should be a piece of rubbish. For those who have never come across the 'Ghost Box' let me explain WHY I was adamantly against it, and why I was its biggest critic! This is also known as the RadioShack Hack: the reason being that you take certain models of hand-held transistor radios (usually RadioShack models) and disable the scanner. This means that now the radio will scan, but not be able to stop at any channels it may find, therefore continuously scanning up and down the bandwidth producing radio snippets and white noise as it goes. This is great, but to me rather ludicrous, if for no other reason than any claimed evidence is already tainted by the fact it does work with radio snippets. There are a hundred responses that could fit our questions and we could claim were answers, when in fact they were just radio station voices innocently coming through. Hopefully by now you are seeing why my critical-thinking mind was VERY against this device, and still is. No matter what happened, this could never be put forward in any credible manner. Here are my original thoughts as written on our forum:

"The RadioShack Hack is based on the same concept as Franks Box. Franks Box was built by Frank Sumption after he supposedly channelled through Edison, who just happened to pick Frank to finish off his design on a device he was working on to contact the dead. Frank was supposedly told that only 30 people worldwide would be able to use it.

However, if you delve into the truth... There is no record of Edison ever building this device and in fact more evidence to point to the fact that he was sceptical of the paranormal in general. Apparently, the Edison Museum states that they are being constantly bombarded with requests for this paper of Edison's that doesn't exist. This is all based on one of Edison's comments in an interview with a well-known reporter of the time. However, what is conveniently missed out is that he gave another interview soon after where he had admitted to have been only toying with this reporter because he had annoyed him. He had become quite surprised that what was said had ever been taken seriously.

So that is the dubious history of Franks Box. Now... onto why we don't and can't use it. This device is designed to work on pink/white noise etc and is set up to scan quickly through AM bandwidth. As you can imagine the AM bandwidth is teeming with radio signals from not just here but from overseas too in foreign languages. By this very fact alone, a person has already corrupted any evidence they may have received and so it could never be taken credibly. Statistics are that when skipping through the bandwidth, they are always going to pick up quick words that they are going to be able to place as an answer to their questions. Like pareidolia in photos (where the brain matrixes visual patterns), their minds will also try and fit these audio signals into what we are expecting or wanting to hear."

So there you have it – my views on 'the Ghost Box'!

However, I am reluctantly going to write about it here. I will let you make up your own minds. This is merely another curiosity in the many experiments we conduct, and it must be remembered that we DO NOT use this officially as P.F.I. research... yes, I AM stressing that a lot in this chapter!

A New Chapter in Experiments

"OK, since this is NOT going away anytime soon," I wrote in our forum after yet another post about the Ghost Box, "I will announce now that P.F.I. will be doing six months of work with this thing and we will let you know our findings". I reluctantly threw the gauntlet down and had full intentions of disproving this thing and putting the puppy to bed once and for all. I already had assumptions on what would happen and what we would find, and was confident of what my final answer would be. Assumptions are funny things.

"I hope you enjoyed it," I smiled at the evening's tour as they departed. I watched Spils shut and lock the door and I sighed with relief as, not long before the end of the tour, I had been hit with symptoms of gastro but, as they say, the show had to go on. It had become a very long and uncomfortable last half hour made longer due to many of them wanting to hang back and chat.

"Right then… I am off!" I scooted rapidly to the room most needed at that moment.

Meanwhile it was decided that Anna and Spils would fire up the Ghost Box in the Gaol for the first time, and the old metal staircase leading up to the Governor's quarters in the laneway was chosen as the spot. Whilst sitting, I vaguely heard noise from outside but didn't think anything of it – after all they weren't going to get anything except probably sports reports and talk back shows!

It wasn't long though, before I heard hurried footsteps approaching the shop as if somebody was in a panic. As my bout had passed for now, I held my stomach and went to see what it was about. Anna was standing there wild-eyed, rapidly talking and making no sense at all. Slowing her down she finally told me that whilst I was otherwise engaged, they had turned the Box on. The first spoken sentence had been: "You shouldn't be here!" followed sternly by the same voice, "We shouldn't be having this conversation!" This had spooked Anna and she had come running back to get me.

"Go on then… turn it on," I stood now by the stairs myself, arms folded in that disbelieving, 'daring-it-to-do-something' stance.

The model that we were working with runs through the stations rapidly, each time it registers one it will click before moving on. All I was hearing this night were the clicks and snippets of radio, nothing more.

"Pretty much as expected," I sighed in that way when you needed others to know you were right!

Feeling slightly awkward now, Spils spoke up: "Hey guys, if you are there, Alison doesn't believe in any of this." He paused and looked around before returning to finish his sentence, "Just to let her know you are here, can you possibly say her name... Alison?"

The clicking continued for a few seconds longer before it abruptly halted and silence ensued momentarily: then a strong clear male voice rang out: "Alison." With that the radio started scanning again and the now familiar clicking could be heard once more.

Spil's laughed at me triumphantly and hit the air… "Niiice!"

Keeping my poise and my arms folded, I stared at the box, "Coincidence," I said simply.

He tried some more questions in the hope of eliciting another response from it, but for now the radio had stopped being co-operative as had my stomach, so we thought we best call it a night and go home.

Driving home I did think back on the incident. What Anna heard, I couldn't comment on, after all I didn't hear it myself and I was still convinced it was nothing but coincidental radio snippets. But, my name being spoken? I hadn't let on at the time, but it had just raised my curiosity. It puzzled me that it sounded different to the radio snippets that we had been listening to. What also made me curious was the fact that the radio had come to a halt from scanning when the name came through before starting up once more.

'Ok Spils,' I thought to myself, 'you have got your wish, we will now trial this as a team'.

—o0o—

And so here we were on our first big investigation back in the Adelaide Gaol. The team this night only consisted of Spilios and myself, and our chief aim had been to come in and assess the Eight-Ball noise that we had captured. We had managed to do this to our own satisfaction, and now it was time to move on to another section of the Gaol – and where better than the New Building.

Upon entering the New Building that night, we noted how it felt very different. The atmosphere felt thicker and, although not unwelcoming, it did have a feel of unease to it that we had not experienced for quite some time. Strangely we had been in there only an hour earlier and it had felt very comfortable then. As we wandered through to 'A' Wing, we paused and looked at each other. Several of the doors were now wide open, not unusual under normal circumstances, except that we had spent time earlier turning off lights and closing all the cell doors. A thrill passed through us... maybe we would have a good night after all.

Quickly shutting the doors once more we proceeded to set up the equipment close to the Condemned Cells. As we chatted there was a creaking sound that came from the Solitary Cell down the end of the block. Turning, we saw that it was now open once more. "Wind," I shrugged. But even so we decided we would go down and inspect it. With an Ambient/wind meter in hand we entered the cell, taking wind velocity measurements as we went. Nothing.

"Maybe hold it closer to the upper window," Spils suggested.

Standing on the wooden bed I held it up against the now-neglected window that once held thick soundproof glass. Nothing.

"It still could have been wind," I suggested as I climbed back down.

Standing in the cell quietly for a while longer, there was now very little movement. The door remained still. Holding the meter closer to the door, I started to take the wind speeds.

"If there is anybody there," Spils spoke from behind me, "can you open the door for us guys?"

No sooner had Spils said this, than the door started to creek open slowly. "Nice," Spils started to laugh whilst steadying the video camera that he was holding.

"Nothing is registering on the wind meter," I said studying the display on the meter that was still reading 0.

But Spils's smile broadened even wider upon leaving the Solitary Cell, to find that the main door had silently opened too. Strange, as this door was directly next to the Solitary Cell we were occupying, and there had been a carefully-placed brick pressed hard against it... a brick that noisily grated across the cement when the door is opened. Although directly next to it, we had heard nothing.

But once again things settled; doors went quiet and we proceeded to continue setting up. Trigger objects were carefully placed on the floor, consisting of items that may appeal to prisoners or even guards: a cigarette, a bottle of beer and nice shiny coins.

"Shall we try the Ghost Box?" Spils asked eagerly. Grimacing, I nodded and watched as he pulled out the small white device and set it up. I was still far from convinced, and half of me still couldn't believe I was even contemplating trying this out once again. 'Well, Spils can ask the questions,' I thought to myself. I still felt too uncomfortable and foolish speaking to a radio!

Again at this point I am going to stress that this is NOT being presented as evidence of dead people talking through the radio. Yes, my rational thinking is still at work here as is my scepticism. However, as a curiosity I will note what happened next, and then it is up to you, the reader, to make up your own mind.

Our first attempt was in 'B' Wing at the foot of the stairs. We appeared to get nothing for the short time we were running it, except the expected random radio snippets.

As we sat in 'A' Wing quietly listening to the radio clicking through the stations, Spils began to feel uncomfortable. As Spils was obviously not going to take the first step at asking the questions, I sighed and decided to begin… "Is somebody here with us tonight?"

It was at that precise moment that the main door with the brick against it chose to slide open causing Spils to jump up quickly, laughing nervously as he did so. As he hovered over me I remained seated and reassured him that nothing was going to happen. "A freak breeze," I suggested.

Listening back, a female voice is clearly heard on the Box: "Get up!" Was this because I remained seated?

After nerves were settled, a few moments later I enquired about the door opening: "I did it," a male voice seemingly answered.

"If there is anybody here," I continued, "and I am not talking to a radio… can you say my name… Alison?"

It should be noted that at the time we did not hear any response at all. But upon listening back to this question on audio, a very clear and haunting female voice seemingly echoes through the building: "Yes… Alison."

Maybe if I had heard this it would have made it easier to ask further questions; but still feeling foolish, I quietened and hoped that Spils would take over. It would appear that Spils either felt as foolish as I did, or he was revelling in my new-found curiosity and remained quiet.

"Do you have a name?" I continued.

An old croaky, but very powerful voice cuts through the radio chatter: "Dugod" (or "Ducat").

Meaning nothing to us at this time, I continued and started questioning about the door once more.

"Who was it who opened the door… or was it just the wind?" I asked.

Listening back we had three different responses: "Wind!" a female cut across almost immediately. "I didn't," another female said more quietly. "She touched it," a male said accusingly.

Moving on I ask, "Is Charles O'Leary here?" A male responded quietly, "He's in prison".

Suddenly the same haunting female voice cut in to the radio noise: "A man is here!"

An authoritative male voice followed moments later: "Leave!"

With this response I asked it to be clearer if it wanted us to leave, and the familiar scraping noise of the brick is heard as the main door creaked open behind me. Interestingly, on listening back to the audio, a male voice is heard to whisper, "Get out!" just as the door opens.

"A creaking door isn't good enough," I said.

At the time we didn't hear some of these responses and so we assumed that we were receiving nothing at all. Deciding that we had run the Box long enough

Ghosts of the Past

and would be better off doing normal monitoring, Spils announced that we were going to turn it off.

Spils: "See you." "Alison," an old croaky voice replied. This was closely followed by a female voice, "G'bye".

With this the Ghost Box experiment was brought to a close and we continued our investigation as we normally would. By then, however, calm had settled over the Gaol once more for the night.

It is at this point I am going to add an update to the above responses. As I was sorting through my thousands of photos taken at the Gaol for this book, I came across ones showing the graffiti etched into the external brickwork of the New Building. One in particular caught my attention. There it was… Duguid or Dugud! Could this be the same person referred to in the recording, or just coincidence? If so, who was this Duguid? Sadly we may never know! Once more all we are left with is just a curious mystery.

—ooo—

The name 'Duguid/Dugud' etched into the brickwork.

A New Chapter in Experiments

"OK, now you have my curiosity," I admitted to Spils over the phone. Listening back to the audio, I now discovered the voices and the apparent responses that we had missed whilst listening live. "I am still not convinced," I added hastily, "but we need to run it again".

And so it was that days later we were back in the Gaol once more.

Setting up the experiment exactly as before, we positioned ourselves close to the same trigger objects that we had placed in 'A' Wing and sat quietly for a moment before I nodded and we switched the Box on.

This time Spils took up the role of questioner and began by attempting to get confirmation that we might have somebody with us. He did this by asking the normal range of questions including saying our names, which seemed to elicit a couple of 'Alisons', but nothing that was as definite as before.

"Guys, to make sure we are talking to you," – he motioned to the gaol keys that were sitting by my side, and I quickly handed them over – "can you see what it is I am holding up?" He held the keys out and we waited to see if there would be a reply.

"Of course," a strong male voice cut in; quickly followed by a female voice, "Key".

Slightly surprised, we started to discuss what it had just said, when a third voice cut in almost as if it was late but wanted to get the word in too: "Keys".

"Thanks guys!" Spils smiled politely.

"You're welcome," a quiet voice replied from the radio.

Spils grinned at my now-furrowing brow, but continued the line of questioning. Handing the keys back to me, he then reached into his pocket and withdrew his mobile phone. "OK guys can you see what this is that I am holding up?"

There was a longer pause before the male voice came back through: "No." This was closely followed however by a female voice again, "I think it's a pho…" but her last word faded as the station moved on in the scanning.

"That one wasn't as convincing," I said slowly, "The word was cut off and it could have been leading to something else".

"Phone!" a loud, clear, almost upper-class female voice rang out from the radio just at that moment.

Encouraged that maybe there was something there, we moved on. "Guys, we brought you some gifts," Spils indicated the trigger objects that were to one side of us, "cigarettes, beer and some money. Do you like cigarettes?"

"We don't need them," a young man replies.

It was at this point that the lady appears to come through once more: "He's back," before the authoritative male voice cuts through, "Now leave".

After this all went quiet and all we listened to was mindless radio snippets as the radio ran through its channels.

It is interesting to note at this point, that IF these are the voices of people and not just radio, then there appeared to be a couple of more-playful characters there; at least one of whom appeared to be female. As no females were ever kept in this building – yet a grey lady has been witnessed many times – the question would be: are we dealing with a completely different time period from the Gaol itself? Were earlier settlements discovered under the Gaol floors involved in this?

The third character that often seemed to come through, appeared to be a more authoritative character who seemingly did not like us there. Could this be the guard? Was he still running a working Gaol and felt we had no place there? We had picked up in the first couple of sessions mainly sentences like: "Who are you?", "What are you doing here?", "Leave", "Leave Now", "Out," and "Get out". These seemed to always be captured in the New Building and on the stairs leading up to the guard's office.

On one occasion Spils asked politely, "Sir, what do you like to be called?" A pause before a strong male voice came back to him: "Sir!"

But for this session, all was now quiet. 'Sir' apparently had arrived and everything went silent – apart from constant clicking and sports reports that were issuing forth – so we returned to our usual methodology without further incident.

—ooo—

A New Chapter in Experiments

Before moving on, however, I will leave you with one last incident with this so-called 'Ghost Box'.

This particular night we decided to work in the Remand Centre, and Debbie had joined us for the night. Debbie had been one of the backups at the Gaol, and although she was not a full P.F.I. member at this time, she was an adopted one when working at the Gaol.

Under the glow cast from the automatic sensor light in the museum area, we set up in the Cell Block and waited for the sensor light to turn itself off. Nodding, we set the Box going. Sitting listening to it for a while, we noticed how the atmosphere had begun to change in the block. A slight unease had crept over the area, not uncommon though in this section of the Gaol.

"Guys… if there is anybody there can you confirm by saying one of our names?" Spils started up the questioning, "Can you say my name, Spilios?"

It was then that we had the strongest reply of all – one that made the whole thing more curious to me personally – and why I even risked any credibility at all to put this subject in this book.

A clear male voice rang out: "Spilios."

Now why should this be so curious? Coincidence? Well, according to Spils, his name Spilios is actually a rare Greek name. The only two people that he knows with this name are himself and his Grandfather. For this name to have come through the radio at that precise moment – never mind any other moment – would be incredible. On top of this, if it had been a Greek radio station snippet… the name would have been pronounced without the 's' on the end as that is the true pronunciation of it. In this case it said the name as Spils had spoken it.

One more voice came through, though, as we were chatting to each other. "Beware," it said; before another added, "entity".

With that it seemed to fall back into mindless radio once more.

"Can you guys maybe do something, or come forward and make yourselves known?"

Ghosts of the Past

The Museum where the rustling of clothing was heard

I listened as Spils continued his questioning; but with my legs now cramping up, I decided I would wander over to the arched doorway and take some photographs through into the museum. So there I stood taking a couple of flash photos. I was about to shoot a third when I hesitated. Did I just hear that, or was it imagination? I was sure I had just heard movement at the far end. The rustling of clothing. Yes, there it was again! The subtle sound of clothing rubbing was coming from the far end of the block. Frustratingly, the large interactive displays were blocking my vision of the cause of the noise. At this point it hadn't occurred to me that if somebody had been there, the sensor light by rights should have turned on by now. I raised my camera once more and took another photograph. In response the noise seemed to get louder, but not in a getting-closer way, just more intense. Peering harder into the gloom and starting to feel unnerved, I imagined I saw a shadow moving in the green glow cast by the Exit sign light. Backing up slowly I went to join Spils and Debbie to warn them. I was convinced at this point that what we may be dealing with was an intruder in the Gaol: there was no thought of 'ghosts'. This had been a very real noise.

Finally, joining back up with the others, I indicated with a finger for them not to react and whispered: "Somebody is here." My aim at this point was not to alert the intruder that we were aware of his presence, I really wanted to catch him out. It was then, as Spils and Debbie looked at me and then towards the Remand museum, that the area was suddenly flooded with light as the sensor light came on.

Leaping to our feet we grabbed our cameras and ran towards the entrance, zigzagging our way through the displays until we reached the open metal door that led out into the Turning Circle… nothing. It was empty.

"Lock down the yards!" I called out to them as I went to look down the alleyway… still nobody. The idea being, that if we locked down areas of the Gaol we could then unlock and search them one by one, that way he had nowhere to go. Hesitantly we went into each yard, camera at the ready: after all if Spils was going to be attacked by the intruder, and yes, it was Spils we chose to go first, we would at least have evidence of the attack. Every corner of the Gaol was searched and every cell – but nothing. Much to my surprise there was absolutely no indication at all of an intruder, even though I had been convinced we would find one. There was just no place for him to go.

Returning back to the Remand we did notice the area felt more at peace than before. That unease had left, and the night now seemed to promise nothing. We waited a while longer but it was now obvious that nothing more would happen. Had we had our chance? If we had not assumed it was an intruder, and so broken the moment by doing the search, would it have built and something else happened? Had it come forward and been a more physical presence after Spils asked for this? Sadly we will now probably never know.

The entrance to 'C' Wing New Building.

Chapter 12
What of the Future?

> *"Whilst watching the video in the Remand Centre, I felt uneasy and a mysterious chill kept blowing back and forth until it stopped right in front of me. I was then touched on the back twice, but there was nobody behind me. I then felt as if I couldn't move, then was pushed up against the wall."*
>
> (Constance, Ghost Tour)

So it is that we draw to a close on this book: but is it the end? No, I don't feel it is. I believe this Gaol has many more experiences to offer yet, to both us as a team and to the general public at large. It has certainly been an interesting and exciting journey so far, a journey that hasn't finished yet though, I feel.

As our methodology evolves and changes there is much more we can do here. More theories to be tested and more patterns to be found. And, as always, just when we think we have some sort of definite idea, we know from past experience that she will throw something at us to turn that idea upside down and put us back to stage one, once more! She seemingly likes to play that way.

It has to be remembered that all we have are experiences and theories: nothing more. They have ranged from the simple thinking of 'deceased people still haunting the place', through to 'we ourselves are somehow manifesting this'. One thing I have moved on from is the idea that it is ALL natural or simply imagination. Certainly a lot of it we have dismissed as natural phenomena over the years – and I have managed to debunk most of our own photos, and actually felt good about doing so – but there is a lot that has happened there that cannot be dismissed so easily. Will we find a natural answer eventually? Maybe. But for now, some of it still remains a bit of a mystery, and we all love a good mystery don't we?

It is at this stage I would like to point out once more, that this book is only intended to share our experiences with you, not to make claims or try to give 'proof'. For this reason we have not gone into techniques or our true methodology

Ghosts of the Past

as most of you reading this would probably find it tedious to wade through. It is simply a record of one team's experience in this fascinating old building. It is also intended to maybe share the beauty and the love that we hold for this building with you. Hopefully those who read this will appreciate her a little bit more and help you to treasure the history she has on offer. She has lots of interesting stories to tell, both historically and of the more 'ghostly' kind. Hopefully you will come and visit her to hear some of these for yourself. We can't promise you a ghost… we wish! But, we can promise you an enriching experience.

In April 2010, at the time I was putting the finishing touches to this book, the tours and investigations had been quiet for some months. Another hot and dry summer had come to a close and a peace had settled over the Gaol. It would appear from our eight years of keeping records that this phenomenon apparently goes through cycles. During hot dry weather it has been noted that it seems weaker and sometimes almost non-existent. And with this in mind I will tell you two last stories before we close.

—o0o—

The first occurrence happened on a tour during the time as I was writing a 'final' chapter. As normal I stood in front of the eager crowd and apologized: "Sorry guys, we can't promise you a ghost tonight…as you can imagine the paranormal doesn't quite work like that." I went on to explain that if we could promise a ghost each and every time, then we would be incredibly rich and the building wouldn't be in such disrepair in areas. "In fact," I went on, "I will be honest and say that it has been REALLY quiet in here the last couple of months". Famous last words!

I was first aware of something happening as we reached the New Building. There I stood, third step up on the old metal staircase and started the story telling for that particular area. I had become aware that there was an unsettled feeling amongst a small group of the people. They had started to talk quietly amongst themselves; and an insecure voice started to tell me: 'Oh no… I am boring them!' But they soon settled once more and it wasn't until the end of the tour that I found out what had transpired there.

"Something touched me," a girl said quietly, "right here!" She pointed to the side of her leg and her upper thigh.

She went on to describe how something seemingly had rubbed her very firmly at that point, just to one side of the lower buttock. Anna, who had been concentrating on the money looked up. She pointed to the area on her own thigh and related how she too had felt this before, and how she had awoken the next morning to find a bruise showing there. We did ask the girl to let us know if she found the same thing the next morning, but as often is the case, they leave and we hear no more from them.

Two days later I received an email from a lady named Sarah. She had been on this particular tour also and was thrilled with it and wanted me to know. The reason she was so thrilled? Apparently she had arrived home that night to find her husband, who had also been on the tour, was rather distressed. Asking what was wrong, he went on to explain how he had been in the Induction Centre exploring when, in a certain point of the building, he had been grabbed on the arm by something unseen. It had been a strong grip and felt icy cold on the skin. This had shaken him up, but he had not wanted to mention it on the tour. The reason? Because he was a full sceptic and this went against everything he believed. The lady was so grateful as now, because of this tour, he was far more open to this subject: one that she had wanted to share with him for a while.

On these tours, I joke about how it is mainly only the 'manly' men who get grabbed in the building. "If you don't get grabbed," I call after the crowd as they disappear through the dark doorway, "then you are just NOT manly enough!" On this occasion I told Sarah to congratulate her husband, as we hadn't had anybody grabbed since our investigator, and that he should pat himself on the back and be proud… he was obviously VERY manly!

—ooo—

The last event I want to relate occurred on Friday, 16 April 2010 about 11.30pm. "Was that a train going by?" The gentleman from the tour looked at me in surprise.

"Erm… No!" I found myself replying from the open doorway of one of the cells, where I had involuntarily just placed myself.

The main tour had left and, as I had missed out on listening to our Electronic Voice Phenomena (EVP) samples while assisting my back-up elsewhere, I had taken a couple of people back to the New Building so they could catch up on what the others had been allowed to listen to. As we stood discussing the paranormal, we fell silent as we strained to listen: What was that faint rumble coming from the other side of the building? The rumble rapidly grew in intensity. Looking up we braced ourselves as a sound – similar to that of a freight train charging across the whole second floor of the building – caused the old cell doors to groan and move in their frames before, finally, all was silent once more.

"Earthquake?" I suggested, although it hadn't gone amiss that we had felt nothing through our feet, nor had we heard any of the noise flowing through the lower floor. Whatever it was, we were pretty excited though!

Fifteen minutes later we were bidding our final guests farewell and I quickly pulled out my phone to text Spilios, our team member, and simply typed: "O.M.G!"

"What, the Earthquake?" was the reply seconds later. Puzzle solved: nothing odd or paranormal about the event after all… or was there? Feeling a little deflated I tapped back: "No, the activity that happened BEFORE this!"

For a while now I have been meaning to write an article on a certain topic, and this earthquake was the perfect inspiration to finally make that start. The Subject? Does seismic activity have any affect at all on the paranormal, or on our perceptions of what is paranormal?

It was by pure chance that I came to be standing in the most 'active' building in the Adelaide Gaol at the very moment that Adelaide experienced its first sizeable earthquake in twenty years – a chance that I felt most grateful for. How many investigators have had the opportunity to be in a supposedly 'haunted' location at the time of seismic build-up? How many have also had twenty guinea pigs to monitor in the form of a public Ghost Tour at the same time? No, this was certainly my lucky night in some respects: but not in others. The drawback being, that because I was officially conducting a 'tour' and not an 'investigation', we had no equipment running at the time! So the following can only be put forward as an observation: nothing more.

It had been a strange night in the Gaol even before the tour arrived. There was an air of unease; one that I never let get to me too often in there, but I put it to one side and continued to prepare for the tour. Debbie, my back-up for the night, came with me to check that all cell lights were off and the Hanging Tower door was shut, though not locked. Our route took us into the Remand Centre, a two-part block with a secluded exercise yard off to one side. As Debbie walked down one side of the well-lit museum section to shut the door leading out into the yard, I took a step into the gloom of the actual two-storey cellblock. It was then I abruptly came to a halt, for I heard footsteps issuing from down the other end.

What of the Future?

Not clear steps, but ones with a shuffling nature to them. Backing up a little, I forgot about the step that lay behind me and ended up assuming a much different view of the block – from my back, with my legs kicking wildly into the air – much to the mirth of Debbie, I might add. But I could still see down the block, and there was no further movement. I picked myself up and we walked in to make sure there was nobody hiding. We walked along the bottom floor, searching the darkened cells, our torchlight dancing off walls and under beds as we strolled through. Nothing! It should be noted that I had not been startled by the thought that the footsteps were a 'ghost', but that maybe we had an intruder in the Gaol, which we have had several times before. As we could now hear cars arriving, we decided we should move back to the shop.

As I went to let a car through the gates, it stopped and the driver wound the window down: "Hello Alison, do you remember us?"

"Not in the dark!" I said apologetically, peering at the silhouettes that sat in their car.

They reminded me that they were a couple I had met on a previous tour and who I had talked to a couple of times on the phone. With this in mind, just before I started the tour, I asked if they would be happy to go with Debbie and check the Remand Centre for an intruder once and for all. I was to remain behind and start the tour.

Interestingly the tour seemed edgy that night. They too seemed to be picking up on the atmosphere which was decidedly unpleasant and felt more menacing than usual. My tours are usually designed for fun: after all I can't promise them a ghost, but I can ensure they go away feeling like they had a great night. For this reason it was unusual for a tour to be getting SO edgy. Their unease only grew as Debbie and the couple returned. It was obvious something had happened, and now the tour wanted to know everything… after all, this was happening live folks!

Debbie and the guests told how they had re-entered the Remand Centre and walked down both sides of the museum, passing both doors to the yard as they went. On entering the Remand Cellblock… footsteps had been heard. Again these were described as shuffling steps, only this time they were coming from the floor above. Checking the gate to the stairs was still locked, they knew if there was an intruder there was no escape for him. Carefully they unlocked the gate and climbed the stairs. Each cell was checked, but there was no intruder and nowhere for him to hide. Finally, giving up on the search, they headed back to rejoin the

Ghosts of the Past

The gate to the Remand Centre cells.

tour. It was as they were walking back through the museum that Debbie's jaw dropped in surprise. A door stood wide open out to the secluded yard… a door that hadn't been used in years and that had been bolted shut moments earlier. What mystified her even more was the fact that to unbolt this door and shove it open, a lot of noise had to be produced. Their time in the cellblock had been one of silence!

The tour nervously bunched closer together, and even though the yards were well lit, a couple of people were clearly on the verge of panic. I have to admit that I too was fighting a feeling of dread; a feeling that had long since become a stranger to me for many years now.

But why did this night have a completely different atmosphere? Why were people feeling unusually fearful and uneasy, including myself. Why were people reporting having seen things and felt things as they were walking through, including one lady who had her ear whistled into?

What of the Future?

It was after we waved goodbye to the tour and the four of us had returned to the New Building, that the earthquake struck!

Could it be that the energy involved with seismic activity, also affects the activity we regard as paranormal? It would appear that it certainly was making people feel more nervous.

But this also brings me to another theory of a more natural explanation. With seismic activity and thunderstorms comes another phenomena: infrasound – sounds that are lower than our hearing ability. Elephants, whales and other animals communicate with such sounds. It is also thought that this is how animals can avoid the danger of earthquakes due to hearing these low infrasound rumbles.

There is another interesting thing about this subject: experiments have shown that when the human brain is subjected to these sounds it can produce symptoms similar to those that people report with hauntings – including fear, paranoia and the feelings of being watched.

Could this have been the real cause of our fear that night? It certainly would be a simple explanation, and a comfortable natural one. But then, of course, there is the question of the footsteps and the opening of bolted doors!

—000—

And so it is here that I will finish our tales. I suspect that with this last story, comes a new beginning. A new cycle to explore and maybe a new chapter in the Gaol's possibly 'haunted' history is about to begin.

I hope you have enjoyed this book as much as I have enjoyed recounting our tales. Hopefully we will see you visiting the Adelaide Gaol very soon.

The outer wall with loose brickwork designed to prevent prisoners from escaping.

Chapter 13
A Final Farewell

It has now been 3 years since this book was published and was originally intended only as a record of one teams' adventures in this beautiful and historic building. It was printed as a small run, and sold in only two outlets, the Adelaide Gaol and my own websites. However, it has turned out for whatever reason, to be fairly popular and despite its small circulation and lack of marketing; it has still managed to sell over 350 copies to date. It is now ready for a reprint which gives me the opportunity to conclude this book with a few extra stories and experiences which we have gathered over the last two years before finally bringing our journey to a close once and for all.

A NEW VENTURE—"Do you do any other tours?" a guest on an Adelaide Gaol tour asked me one day. Slowly I shook my head, "No, I don't know of any others here in Adelaide."

The first time this question was asked a seed had been planted in the back of my mind. Many questions later, this seed finally started to germinate until towards the end of 2009, it slowly started to make its way to the surface.

"Alison, would you like to conduct paranormal workshops?" The President of the A.G.P.S. had already brought this up several times, helping move my decision forward on possibly setting up my own ghost tour business. After all, with over 8 years of tour guiding experience and having researched the subject of the paranormal since 1989, it seemed a natural step to combine my two loves together.

It was after this question was presented one more time that I finally showed the President a proposal outlining what I wanted to submit to D.E.N.R. regarding the conducting of workshops in the Gaol. I pointed out that largely it would be intended as a business for me, but one that would also bring added revenue and exposure to the Gaol and their own tours there. In return for A.G.P.S. co-operation, I was quite prepared to hold several paranormal workshops a year for them and, with the help from their volunteers, would donate the entire profit of these to the A.G.P.S.

The President silently read through what I was proposing. Finally, putting her cigarette out, she nodded and agreed that she could see no problem with this proposal and even thought it a good idea, especially with the AGPS set to benefit from it. So it was that D.E.N.R. was to receive the proposal soon after.

The road ahead was still not smooth however, as we were having yet another change of management and priorities were not with potential new contracts at that time. During the wait however, the name of the business needed to be established. Should it be under the Paranormal Field Investigators banner? I decided in reality P.F.I. was very much my serious research side and this business was to be more entertainment and storytelling, although keeping all the stories very real. I knew there would be a certain element out there that would condemn us as a paranormal group running tours should P.F.I be involved. No, I decided, this was my journey and not P.F.I.'s so it had to be kept very separate.

What to name it then? It was many coffees later and still with no names coming to mind that felt right, that I glanced at my computer screen and wondered if Google could help. A site for band naming came up where you could punch in a word and it would spit out an appropriate band name. Ok, well if it works for bands then it should surely be of some help for a business name, so I punched in the word 'ghost'. Immediately it spat out 'Haunted Horizons'. I pondered a moment and tested how it sounded. 'I like it' I thought to myself, a smile now playing on my face. And so, from a random band name generator, Adelaide's Haunted Horizons finally broke through and came into existence. Now all we needed was a tour venue.

"It has been accepted" Bryn Troath, our new Gaol Manager looked up at me from his computer as I hovered in his doorway one day. "We still have to make up the contract for you to sign, but you will have your tour."

Bryn had come into the Gaol only a couple of months earlier and was at first slightly aloof. The easy banter I had enjoyed with the other managers was a little more difficult to establish in the beginning. However the more I got to know this man over time the less nervous I became on approaching him and soon a much easier relationship was established and greatly enjoyed. As I came

A Final Farewell

to understand this gentleman more I also came to admire him, especially when often and under difficult circumstances, he kept his professionalism at all times and only ever followed a path that would benefit the Gaol. In fact during his time there he has definitely made a huge difference to the Old Girl as she has never looked so good or been so popular. The amount of time and effort he put in was to be commended and we should all be very proud of what he has achieved there to date as should he.

It was because of these perceived benefits to the Gaol that my contract was put forward by Bryn to his superiors. He clearly saw that the extra income and promotion could only benefit the Gaol as a whole, although it was always made clear by him that this was simply a trial for one year and that it was only due to my firm knowledge on the security and OH&S procedures in the Gaol that they were even considering it.

That day I went home grinning… the business had its name and now its first venue.

—oOo—

"Ok are we ready?" I slid off the rail that I had perched myself on with Anna, as we sat excitedly waiting for our very first ever guests to arrive. Headlights in the distance were growing brighter as cars approached the gates of the Gaol.

It was Oct 30th 2010, our launch tour at the Adelaide Gaol, and what better night then Halloween! We had a modest group this night which consisted of 3 couples and another small group of friends… not bad for our first tour. We were awaiting the last group and now a car was fast approaching. As with the arrival of our other guests, I wandered over to greet them and introduce myself. Two gentlemen got out laughing loudly, slowly followed by their partners who were looking less than impressed with the situation they now found themselves in.

"Oh we don't believe in any of this stuff, we just wanted to scare our partners" the two gentlemen announced pointing at the two young ladies now standing hesitantly to one side. "They had no idea where they were going until now!" they continued, still laughing.

Already formulating a plan in my head as to how we would separate them from distracting the other group, and already judging on how much fun they would be, I leant over to Anna and whispered "They are definitely mine for the night!" We then proceeded to guide our guests through into the interior of the Gaol.

Ghosts of the Past

As we set off for the ghost tour around the Gaol to update our guests on what had been happening over the years, the two gentlemen, Steve and Peter were jocular, revelling in every moment of their partners' nervousness and being the first ones to drag them into the darker confines of the Gaol.

It was during our coffee break before the actual investigation that I noticed Peter had now become a little quieter and his partner Lisa, a little brighter. Words were spoken between them in lowered voices.

"Is everything ok?" I asked.

Slightly embarrassed he admitted that whilst standing at the foot of the metal staircase in 'B' Wing, he had been listening to my stories of the guard with amusement when he had suddenly felt the back of his head being stroked. He had swung around fully expecting to see Steve or his partner Lisa there pulling a prank on him. However, he had turned around only to find the space behind him empty. This had unnerved him somewhat.

As we were winding up our coffee break, I started to split the group into two smaller teams. I handed a two-way to Anna who already had equipment spilling out of every pocket. "I will take the New Building… if you need me just message" I told her brightly.

With that, my small team and I ventured off into the New Building. As we reached the metal staircase I gratefully offloaded all of the equipment I had been carrying and unlocked the gate leading up to the 2nd floor. We slowly climbed the stairs, reaching a whole new darkness on the upper level of the New Building. I quickly gave them a tour in an area that the public seldom get to see, showing them the cells where known prisoners had been kept. As we wandered in and out of the long deserted cells, Steve piped up "I would love to be put in a cell all on my own."

Smiling mischievously at him, I quickly pointed out that this could definitely be arranged. In fact I added that one of our solitary cells downstairs was definitely the best candidate for his new wish. Quickly, we made our way back down to the lower cells and wound our way into 'A' Wing to find ourselves now standing under the gallows. It was decided that before we left Steve to his own devices, we would first all sit in one of the solitary cells for a short time and attempt some EVP work. Still, the two gentlemen were joking and in good spirits due to the uneasiness that their partners were obviously still experiencing… just what they were after!

A Final Farewell

With the ladies settling themselves on the stark wooden bench, leaving Steve and Pete standing, we started the EVP experiment. We didn't really seem to have anything unusual happen. So I reluctantly dragged out the ghost box. I had made it VERY clear that its use was for entertainment purposes only. Although you will never see it on my research site for reasons stated earlier, we do allow it for tours. The tours are seen more as entertainment and not serious research, but they do give people a chance to try out these different gadgets that they see on T.V. and then have the power to make up their own minds. This was made very clear to Steve and Pete before I balanced the ghost box on the seat next to us; however it didn't stop the look of mirth that passed between them.

Not expecting anything but the usual radio chatter I commenced to ask questions. Even after two years of doing this for tours, the discomfort and embarrassment of talking to a radio in front of a group of complete strangers never quite leaves you!

"If there is anybody here tonight" I began, "maybe you would like to speak to us through this device. Maybe you can manipulate it."

We didn't seem to get much until we asked for verification… "Can you say one of our names, can you say Lisa?" A couple of garbled words were heard before a clear "Lisa" sprung forth. As usual when this occurred, a ripple of excitement went through the group and they asked for other names. We did appear to get a Steve and Alison in an unusual space of time. The mirth was quickly taken up by curiosity and Steve and Pete were soon joining in with the questioning.

After a short time we decided to leave Steve in the room on his own whilst Peter and Lisa went into the opposite cell to try their luck there. Steve's partner and I stood patiently chatting out in the wing, leaving Steve to get a real feel for being in solitary with the ghost box as his only companion.

CRASH! Steve was suddenly by our sides once more.

We looked at him curiously before asking what had happened. He quickly told us how he had been sitting on the bench chatting to thin air, when he said a sense of unease had crept over him before he had felt tapping on the bench followed by subtle movement as if somebody had been sitting with him. Loving every minute of Steve's sudden discomfort and obviously getting a kick out of the fact that the tables had appeared to have been turned, his wife quickly encouraged him to go back into the cell once more. We shut the two heavy doors and stood back, over dramatically looking at our imaginary watches and pretending to time him, supressing our laughter as we did.

Sure enough a few moments later Steve exploded out of the cell. I have to say at this point that it is quite a unique trick to be able to simultaneously open two doors at once with such force! But Steve managed it beautifully and was obviously too agitated to repeat the experience a third time.

"I turned that ghost box on" Steve nervously pointed back to the cell where the Ghost Box was still clicking through the radio stations spitting out garbage. "I asked if there was anything I could do for them and it said 'Yes... run!' Steve had acted on that advice without hesitation.

On listening back to the audio you can clearly hear the sentence and as he crashes out the door it is followed by yet another voice "leave now" but this is almost drowned out by the sound of the doors crashing open and the peals of laughter that were now coming from his partner who was soaking up Steve's discomfort.

Needless to say they went home with a lot of questions on what just happened and a little more open to possibilities.

—ooo—

In the early days, even though we barely covered costs, we had a policy of conducting our tours on request even if it was for only two people. Our thinking was that you never know who those two people might turn out to be and with the business so young, word of mouth was extremely important to us. One such booking really stood out and we are to this day glad we had this policy set in place.

A gentleman by the name of Nicolas was enquiring if we could possibly see our way clear to conducting a tour at short notice. As they were not local but visiting from Victoria, I agreed to do it rather than let them down.

"I don't think I want to go in now" exclaimed Nicolas, one of the gentlemen that now stood before us. Nicolas was looking up at the Gaol, extreme hesitation now showing on his face.

"You can't be serious," Jay, his partner, looked back at him incredulously "we have just come all this way, and now you don't want to go in?"

A Final Farewell

I glanced at my husband, Michael with amusement before trying to reassure Nicolas that all would be fine.

It turned out to be an interesting night to say the least. Although we had a few curious little things occur on the ghost tour the investigation side appeared to become very quiet for activity... in fact it was so quiet that it was almost embarrassing. As I desperately took them from building to building in the hope of finding something, I had almost given up hope and felt almost sorry for them as they obviously had high hopes when they had first arrived.

I should state here that when setting up Haunted Horizons, I asked myself what I would want from a ghost tour. I decided that what would be most important to me would be that should anything happen, I would want to be assured it was for real and not the tour guides putting it on. For this reason we have taken a slightly different track from other tours... no tacky effects, no dress ups, no over dramatics and definitely no 'put-ons' just to make people believe they have had an experience. This also means though that if nothing happens on the night, and most times it won't... then nothing happens! Welcome to the world of paranormal... they don't perform like circus animals and it doesn't happen all of the time. I wish it did as it would definitely make my job so much easier. This night was no exception.

I finally took Nicolas and Jay to our last port of call which was the Induction Centre. We settled ourselves in the middle section of the building where there were two wooden benches for us to relax and set our equipment down. As we began we had no idea that things were about to change.

At this point I thought I would let Nicolas tell his own story as I always believe that it is more interesting coming from the person who experienced it themselves.

"Real History. Real Frights- Our guide, Alison gave us an experience that I have not encountered on any other tour!

The tour started with a walk around the entire gaol. Straight away I got the feeling that we were being watched. The immense grounds and the stillness set the scene for a night of ghostly encounters. For those that love their history they will surely learn a lot from Alison in regards to the gaol's dark past. From stories about ex-prisoners right through to information on Adelaide's history... you surely get your money's worth.

While walking around (and this was before dark) I thought I could hear voices as well as footsteps. I felt like someone was following the group. However, it was in the museum that I experienced my first paranormal encounter. While Alison and Jay were in the Remand Cellblock I kept hearing footsteps in the museum. Instead of joining them in the wing I instead investigated where the noises were coming from. At the same time Alison and Jay were trying to close one of the cell door slots. After looking around the museum (I couldn't see anything) I decided to join the others in the wing. To my amazement as soon as I reached the wing I could see a hand coming from the cell door slot. This hand forcefully smashed the slot down. You can guess what happened next. I ran for my life. I have never been that scared in my life. Well little did I know what lay ahead for the group. [Note: this was a locked cell and we checked inside and there was nobody in there.]

After the tour we made our way back to the V.J. Room, so called from the days that a Visiting Justice would visit the Gaol. Here Alison played us examples of EVP and voices from the ghost box. After my experience (I was still shaking like mad) these samples just put me further on edge.

Next came the investigation.

The investigation itself lasted around two hours. Here you were able to use equipment to track the paranormal as well as visit any location in the prison. Alison took us to places around the prison which have had vast paranormal events. Alas those places would not be the ones that would make me doubt my own sanity.
The Induction Centre looks to be just another building. But by day or night this indeed is a dark place.

As soon as I entered the building I began to feel light headed. It was like it was an extremely hot day. The temperature gauge at that stage read only 22 degrees. That was all about to change. When we sat down on the bench in the Induction Centre the gauge jumped to over 40 in a little over a few minutes. I then asked if any spirit could lessen the temperature on the gauge. I got a response almost straight away and the gauge dropped by 25 degrees. The group then decided to give the ghost box a go. This is where you ask questions and sometimes you might get a response. I'm not a great fan and neither is Alison, but I will give anything a go once. During this period the temperature gauge read 68 degrees. All the others in the room were now all complaining about feeling light headed.

Alison then asked if anyone present could give us a sign that they were there or touch us. Well they did surely show us they were there. A clear noise was heard in the shower block next to us. It went on for a few minutes. The noise could be best described as footsteps walking through dried leaves. It was the same noise that I had heard all the *night. What made this experience worse though was they kept getting closer and closer. Alison tried to radio her husband so that he could bring the video camera but the walkie talkie stopped working mid-sentence. My nerves were shot at this stage. Thank gawd everyone wanted to leave the room.*

After regrouping outside we checked all the equipment. Both the temperature gauge and walkie-talkies needed their batteries changed. What is weird about this is both of them had been just been refreshed before the investigation. These batteries should have lasted weeks. Another weird thing is another group members recording device stopped when the noises got closer. There was no one near the device. On the way back we heard the jail bell ring twice (Alison stated that it never had happened before) and also the between yards buzzer went off. Very unusual indeed.

Let me state that all the above did happen and is real. No gimmicks or pranks. We have audio evidence that all this took place. Thank you Alison for an amazing night. For one that has been searching for such an experience for years, I owe you and the Gaols guests' big time. This tour is indeed worth it"

~ Nicolas Bishop

This was my first introduction to two very special people, Nicolas Bishop and Jay Couch, who were to go on to become treasured friends both to myself, my staff and to fellow guests who have also had the pleasure to meet them along the way. They have come back on many of my tours now and each time they do, we know we are up for a great night.

—ooo—

Over the short time we operated Haunted Horizons in the Gaol, we had a number of people who came as guests for the night but then left us as friends. They became very special to us at Haunted Horizons and still are. So when it was Anna's birthday I decided to forego a public tour that weekend and instead make it a private tour with all our new friends and without alerting Anna to the real purpose of the night. It just so happened that it was a second staff member's birthday that month too.

Ashley Hall had joined us in May 2011 bringing with him plenty of research experience as he had been in a paranormal team previously. He had newly left this team and was now looking for something new to do in the field. Having chatted on Facebook a couple of times, and seeing that he could be of value to our small team, I decided to meet up with him for coffee and somehow what was intended to be an hour's meet soon became about five as we chatted into the night. It was not long after that he joined our small Haunted Horizons team and he quickly became a valued and fun member of my staff.

The night was secretly arranged and our special guests arrived. Dee, Adam, Linley and Simon Twinning as well as Nicolas and Jay greeted each other as it had been a while since they had all last met and there was catching up to be done. At this point I would express my gratitude to Dee for having baked two wonderful birthday cakes for both Anna and Ash. We even managed to sneak them in unnoticed before commencing the night. Needless to say we pulled the birthday surprise off seamlessly and now it was time to start the night's investigation.

Part way through the night and as Jay was less interested in ghosts and more in the history I took him for a wander around on his own whilst my staff took care of the investigation. It was as I was standing chatting to Jay in the Sally port that I noticed torchlight bouncing its way along the laneway towards us. If it was one of my staff, why had they left the tour? The speed at which the torchlight was getting closer told me that something was wrong.

"Dee has just been thrown out of Cell 13" panted Ash, who had raced to get me. I took one look at the concern on his face and we quickly followed him back to the Remand Centre. By this stage Dee had moved back into the V.J. Room and was visibly shaken by her experience.

As I wasn't present I thought I would let Dee tell her own experience.

"As a repeat visitor to the Adelaide Gaol, with small experiences here and there, I got quite a shock on a recent investigation.

Since I started visiting the Gaol, I have never been a fan of the Remand Centre – it always gives me the heebie-jeebies whenever in there. Now I have even more reason not to want to be in there.

I was a little apprehensive when it was suggested we all go into Cell 13 but there was no way I was going to stay out in the Remand Centre on my own and didn't think sitting in the V.J. Room on my own would be all too fun either. So I went in after everyone else and whilst they settled on the two beds, I stood at the door as I felt a little more at ease as it meant I could leave if I wanted to and make a quick exit were something to happen. A quick exit was certainly on the cards it seems. Just not how I imagined it.

A Final Farewell

We introduced ourselves politely to any presence that may be around and Anna turned the ghost box on. We took turns asking questions but I didn't want to ask anything as I was still feeling very uncomfortable about being in there.

After a little while I started feeling ill to the stomach. I really didn't want to be there. I thought it was just due to the fact of where I was and not liking it. I was about to leave when I felt as if something/someone shoved me in the ribs sending me propelling backwards through the door. I didn't even have a chance to try and grab something to stop myself, it all happened too quickly.

It took me a while to stop shaking and to calm down. I wasn't feeling too comfortable for the rest of the night but no other instances occurred and the Gaol seemed rather quiet after that.

The next day I took a photo of the left side of my ribs where I had a large red mark from the impact of whatever it was that had pushed me.

I am not sure what caused this event to happen, or why it happened to me. I have always enjoyed going to the Gaol (and will continue to go, no bumps and bruises are going to scare me off), but I do find it strange that there was something with such force in comparison to the usual pokes and prods some people get during tours."

~ Dee

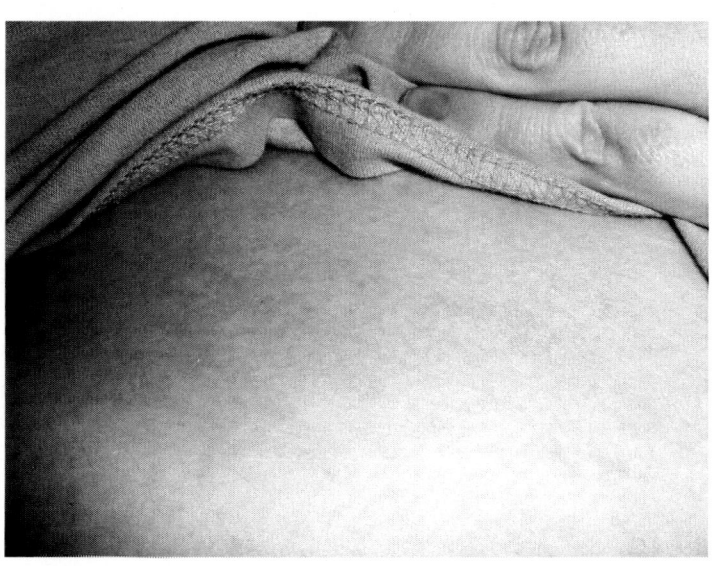

The photo showing the bruising on Dee's side. Sadly black and white does not do it justice.

As an interesting side note. We were running audio and video that night. Although we didn't capture anything on the video apart from the noise of Dee being pushed out of the door (unfortunately Dee was standing just out of camera view) the audio proved to be a lot more curious. At the moment Dee felt herself being pushed, Linley and Simon were asking questions whilst running the ghost box. They appeared not to hear it at the time but on listening back there appeared to be a voice come through.

"Help… help me… please help" came out in succession. Our guests at this point though were talking amongst themselves and had obviously not heard. Could this be the reason for the push? Could it have been sheer frustration at not being heard? Whatever it was, after the incident the whole atmosphere of the block changed and a feeling of peace settled over us once more.

With the night finished, people who had formed friendships through our tours, had to say goodbye to each other once more knowing that it may be a while before they met again. However, it was also tinged with a little sadness for me as a shadow had descended over our future at the Gaol and I was privately aware that we would all meet again, but we may never get to do it again here at the Adelaide Gaol as there was a cloud now hanging over my contract due to disapproval from some of the volunteers.

Ash was also to leave us. For the short time that Ash was with us, both the staff and guests had a lot of fun on the tours. Ash has now moved on and formed his own group, The Paranormal Guide, focusing more on what his first love always was, video making, podcasting and social networking.

—000—

Over the time we operated there as Haunted Horizons, and although we had a few interesting incidents on top of what we have discussed, what was becoming noticeable was how much quieter the Gaol had become. I reflected back over the early days and how statistically we seemed to have more activity and of a stronger nature back in our P.F.I. investigation days. It had certainly seemed to make itself known and felt more in the earlier years then it was presently. Now, you often feel like 'Sir' was there but just wasn't coming forward for whatever reason. It was almost as if they were starting to tire of the circus and constant stream of people trooping through the Gaol each week allexpecting them to perform like circus animals and jump through hoops. Maybe we started as their entertainment, but their entertainment had now become tedious… who knows.

A Final Farewell

Another theory we formulated over time is that often the New Building was quiet with an almost peaceful feel. Then out of the blue, the cycle appears to begin again. Could it be that 'Sir' still follows patterns as he did when alive? Maybe he is still following a roster. and he is only there when in life he would have done 2nd Watch or 'nightshift'. It could also explain why at other times he is reported during the day too.

Sadly at this stage it is a pattern that we won't be following up on so it will remain just an observation as this will possibly be our final farewell to the Gaol both as P.F.I. and H.H. After my 10 years at the Gaol both as volunteer, tour guide and researcher, the biggest change of all blew in and sadly difficulties arose between a couple of Gaol personalities and myself. Unfortunately H.H. was viewed as direct competition, which couldn't be further from the truth, and it appeared that the more popular we became with the public, the worse these feelings grew. Eventually such a fuss was caused that as was feared; D.E.N.R had no choice but to reluctantly discontinue the contract. There were a lot of disappointed people that day when the news came through, both with our regular customers and with the staff, as the tour had become very popular and was receiving excellent feedback. At this point I would like to thank all my customers for their support over that difficult time. It definitely helped light up a dark period for myself and help us to have the confidence that what we were doing was worthwhile and that we should continue which we have done so successfully.

Although I remained as a volunteer at the Gaol and still believe the A.G.P.S. to be a wonderful group of people as a whole, it was with a heavy heart that we conducted our last H.H. Investigation Tour there on the 26th Nov 2011. We were even more saddened that the people on the night, who were raising money for a charity, raved about the tour as they left. We knew we had brought something good to the Gaol… and now it was gone after a successful year of operations there.

—ooo—

"I would like to book a Tailem Town Ghost Tour" the voice on the other end of the phone informed me.

Although the loss of the Gaol was a sad affair, business did not slow and our other venue, Old Tailem Town Pioneer Village was just taking off. Old Tailem Town is owned by Peter Squires, a lovely man who graciously allowed us to at first investigate and then conduct ghost tours in his village. Although it was never a working village, Peter has preserved our history and kept the village authentic by

Ghosts of the Past

purchasing and transporting working buildings and homes, some of which are over 100 years old. Rumours had been rife of ghostly activity for years, especially coming out of the Wolseley Church. We had known about the claims but until this point had never had the opportunity to investigate, largely due to our work at the Gaol. On finally securing permission to investigate, it soon became clear that this could well challenge the Gaol for activity, which surprised us as the Gaol had a much darker history. With unexplained sounds, strange lights, frigid cold spots and finally our witnessing of a dark shadowy figure… this village with its once lived in homes was definitely proving to be an intriguing place.

Yes, it would appear that as one adventure drew to a close another was about to begin!

Old Tailem Town Pioneer Village

A Final Farewell

The Governors Quarters

Ghosts of the Past

BIBLIOGRAPHY

Paranormal Field Investigators Reports, written by Jeff Fausch and Alison Oborn for Paranormal Field Investigators

Inside: A brief History of the Old Adelaide Gaol, Sue Scheiffers, Openbook Print, 2002

South Australia and its Mines, F.S. Dutton, London, 1946

Newspapers of the Day, Trove, National Libraries of Australia

Winner in the SA Tourism Awards and named 'Best Tour Operator' in SA, 2015.

For more information on the Adelaide Gaol and other 'Award Winning' tours run by Alison Oborn and her team at Adelaide's Haunted Horizons, please visit her website at:

www.adelaidehauntedhorizons.com.au
or email alison@adelaidehauntedhorizons.com.au
Visit the Facebook page at www.facebook.com/AdelaideHauntedHorizons